Key to Directions

M000305066

Valley fold

Mountain fold

Fold away from yourself

Fold and unfold to make a crease

Fold exactly in half

Fold exactly in half

Fold so as to join the two circles ○

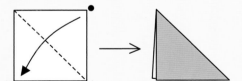

Fold so as to join the two dots ●

Turn over

Enlargement

Rotate

The next drawing shows a different position.
(Level of difficulty)

★ Easy

★★ Standard

★★★ Difficult

15cm×15cm etc.　　Size of paper

×4, ×6 etc.　　Number of sheets
　　　　　　　Number of units

The diagrams next to the drawings of the completed polyhedrons show a three-dimensional view of the framework.

△×8 ☐×6

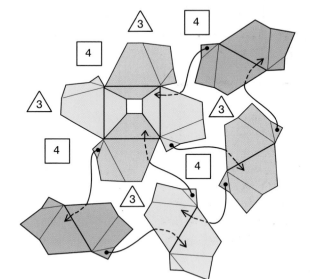

△3 triangles with three sheets

☐4 squares with four sheets

⬠5 pentagons with five sheets

⬡6 hexagons with six sheets

3

contents

Regular Icosahedron /p.12

Cubes /p.9

SQUARE FLAT UNITS

level ★

15cm × 15cm

Assemble by inserting joints into four pockets.

1
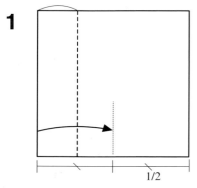

1/2

This width is not fixed.
Fold wherever you like.

2
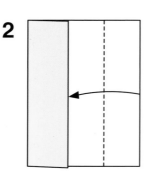

Align the edges.

3
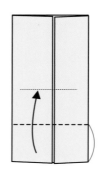

This width is not fixed.
Fold wherever you like.

4
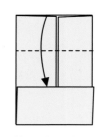

Align the edges.

5

[Assembly Method]

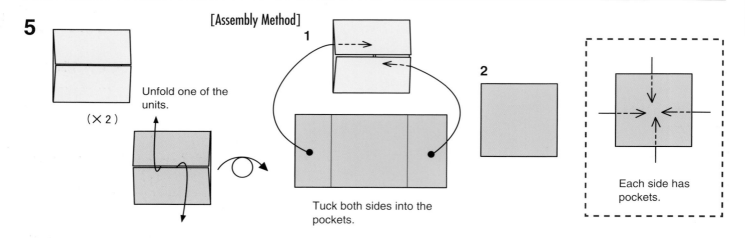

(× 2)

Unfold one of the units.

1

Tuck both sides into the pockets.

2

Each side has pockets.

Joints ● Use Method A for joints, but when the paper is thick or difficult to assemble, use B.

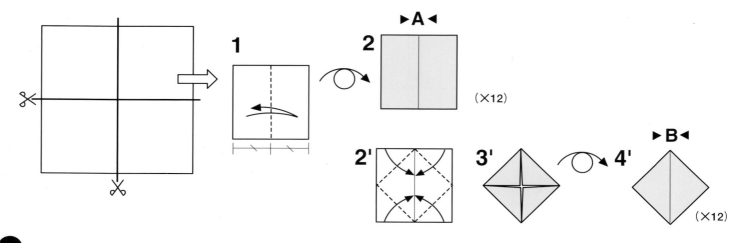

1

2 ►A◄

(×12)

2'   **3'**   **4'** ►B◄

(×12)

CUBE | level ★

15cm × 15cm

Consider the various schematic diagrams.

(×6)

(×12)

The cubes in the photo were assembled using joint B.

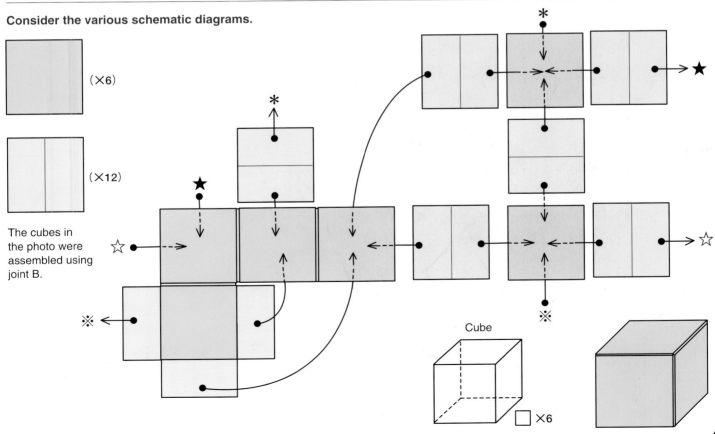

Cube

☐ ×6

The unit has pockets on three sides, and it is assembled by inserting joints into them.

1
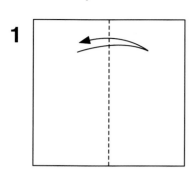

2
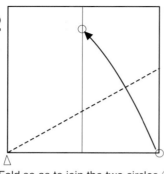

Fold so as to join the two circles ○, using △ as the pivot.

3
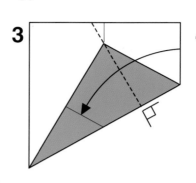

4
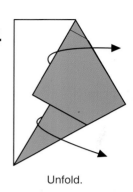

Unfold.

5
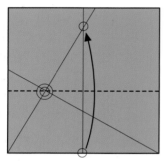

Fold so as to join the two circles ○ at node ◎.

6
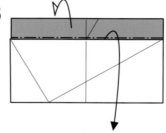

Fold the edge away from yourself and then unfold the upper layer.

7
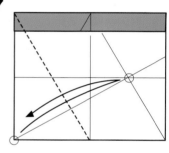

8
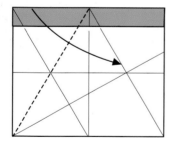

9
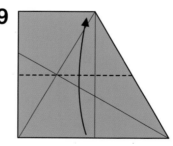

10
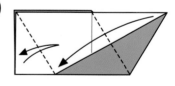

11
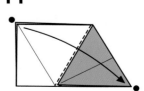

12
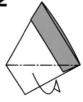

Tuck inside.

13
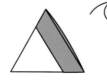

(Back)

14

(Front)

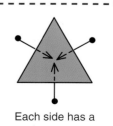

Each side has a pocket.

10

Joint B

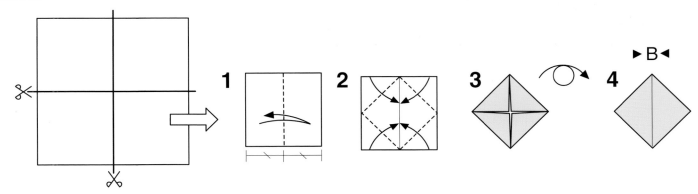

REGULAR TETRAHEDRON | level ★

15cm × 15cm

Equilateral Triangular Flat Unit

Joint B

(×4)

(×6)

[Assembly Method]

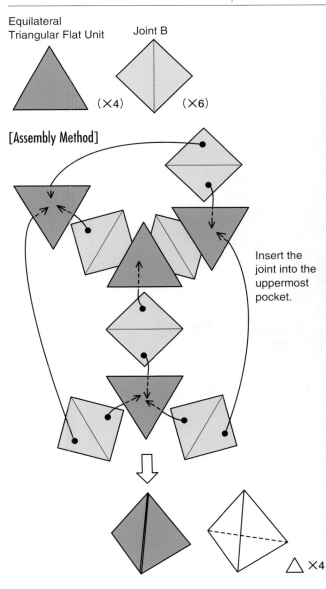

Insert the joint into the uppermost pocket.

△×4

REGULAR OCTAHEDRON AND ICOSAHEDRON | level ★ | 15cm×15cm

Equilateral Triangular
Flat Unit (p.10)

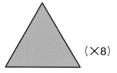 (×8)

Joint B (p.11)

 (×12)

Regular Octahedron

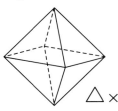

△×8

Equilateral Triangular
Flat Unit (p.10)

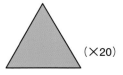 (×20)

Joint B (p.11)

(×30)

Regular Icosahedron

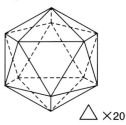

△×20

TRUNCATED REGULAR TETRAHEDRON
Using equilateral triangular flat units.

You can make a regular hexagon by joining 6 equilateral triangular flat units.
It is possible to combine this hexagon with equilateral triangular units.

[Assembly Method]

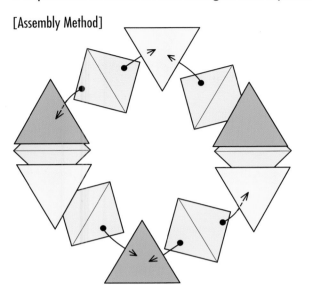

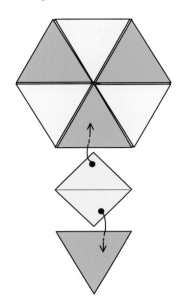

Equilateral Triangular
Flat Unit (p.10)

(×28)

Joint B (p.11)

(×42)

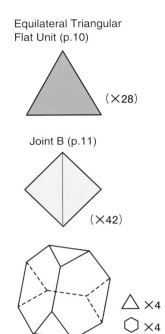

△ ×4
⬡ ×4

2 COMBINATIONS OF SQUARES AND EQUILATERAL TRIANGLES

Squares and equilateral triangles folded from the same size of paper have sides of the same length, and it is possible to connect them. By adding even more components, you can make large, splendid polyhedrons.

ELEMENTS AND FLAT UNITS OF EQUILATERAL TRIANGLE /p.18

REGULAR OCTAHEDRON

VARIANT CUBE /p.17

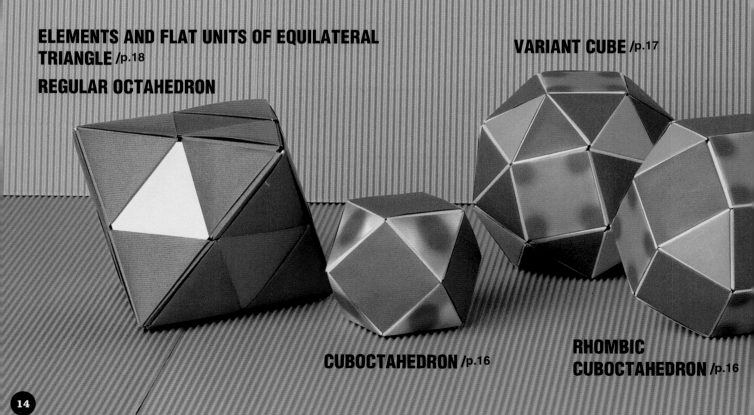

CUBOCTAHEDRON /p.16

RHOMBIC CUBOCTAHEDRON /p.16

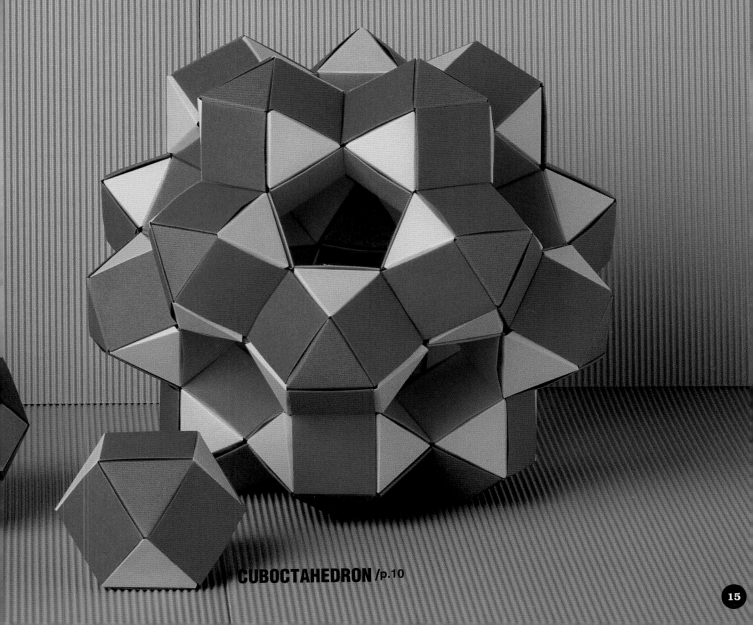

A STRUCTURE MADE OF 20 CUBOCTAHEDRONS /p.21

CUBOCTAHEDRON /p.10

CUBOCTAHEDRON AND RHOMBIC CUBOCTAHEDRON | level ★★ | 7.5cm×7.5cm

Square and equilateral triangular flat units folded from the same size of paper have sides of the same length, and it is possible to join them to make various solids.

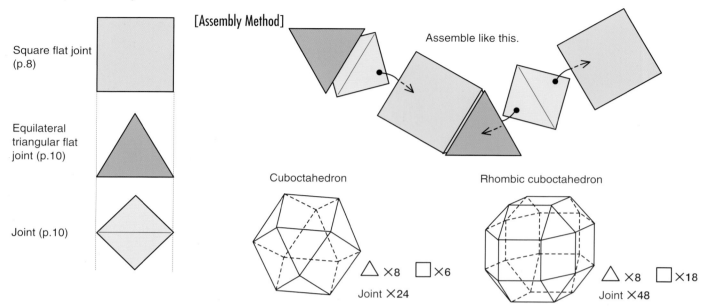

Square flat joint (p.8)

Equilateral triangular flat joint (p.10)

Joint (p.10)

[Assembly Method]

Assemble like this.

Cuboctahedron

△×8 □×6
Joint ×24

Rhombic cuboctahedron

△×8 □×18
Joint ×48

VARIANT CUBE | **level ★★★**

Variant cube

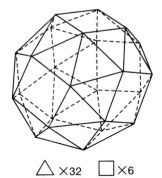

△ ×32   ▢ ×6

Square flat joint (p.8)

(×6)

Equilateral triangular flat joint (p.10)

(×32)

Joint B (p.11)

(×60)

EQUILATERAL TRIANGULAR ELEMENTS AND FLAT UNITS

EQUILATERAL TRIANGULAR ELEMENTS

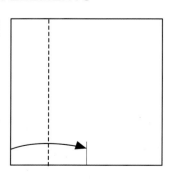

1

2

Make a short crease on the lower side.

3

4

Fold on the crease △ to join the spots marked by the two circles.

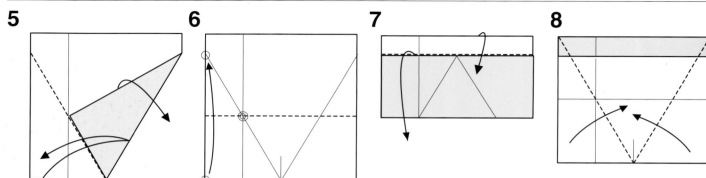

5

6

7

8

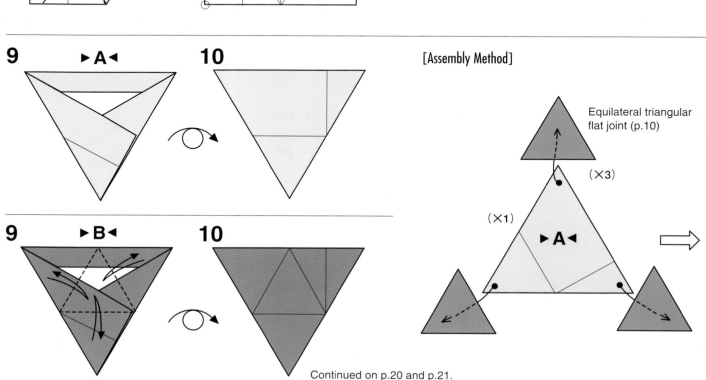

9 ►A◄

10

9 ►B◄

10

[Assembly Method]

Equilateral triangular flat joint (p.10)

(×3)

(×1)

►A◄

Continued on p.20 and p.21.

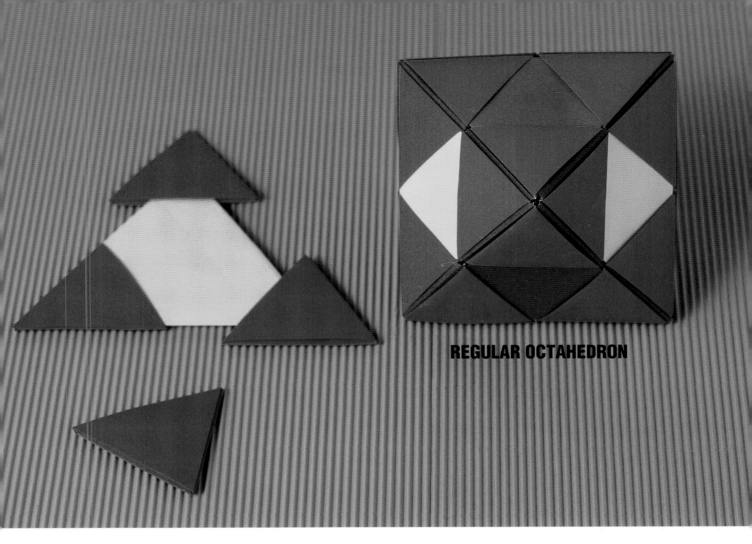

REGULAR OCTAHEDRON

A quadruple equilateral triangle is made by combining 1 equilateral triangular element and 3 equilateral triangular flat units.

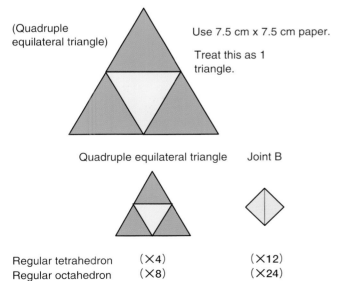

(Quadruple equilateral triangle)

Use 7.5 cm x 7.5 cm paper.

Treat this as 1 triangle.

Quadruple equilateral triangle   Joint B

Regular tetrahedron	(×4)	(×12)
Regular octahedron	(×8)	(×24)
Regular icosahedron	(×20)	(×60)

[Assembly Method]

Joint B (p.11)

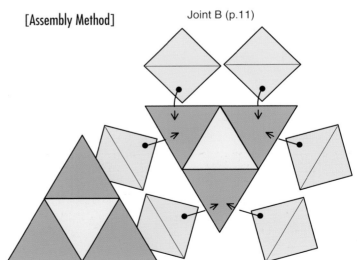

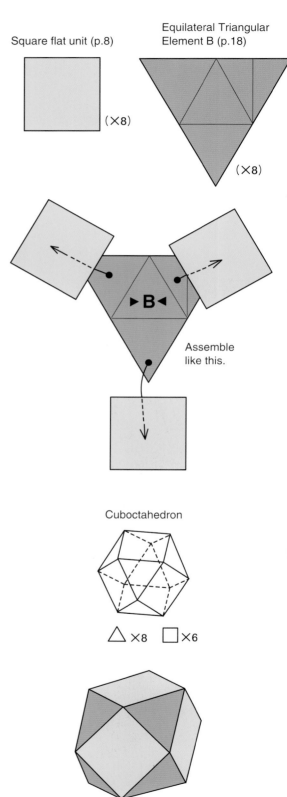

Square flat unit (p.8)

(×8)

Equilateral Triangular
Element B (p.18)

(×8)

▶**B**◀

Assemble
like this.

Cuboctahedron

△ ×8   □ ×6

STRUCTURES MADE OF 20 CUBOCTAHEDRONS | level ★★★ | 8cm×8cm

Square flat unit (p.8)

（×120 : 240 sheets of paper）

5 inside rings of square flat units (orange)   5×12＝60
2 outside square flat units (blue)   2×30＝60

Joint B (p.11)

（×90）

5 inside square flat units   5×12＝60
2 outside square flat units   30

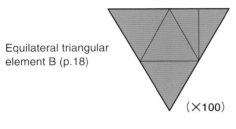

Equilateral triangular element B (p.18)

（×100）

Inside triangles (yellowish green)   20
Outside star-shaped triangles (yellow)   5×12＝60
Exterior triangles (purple)   20

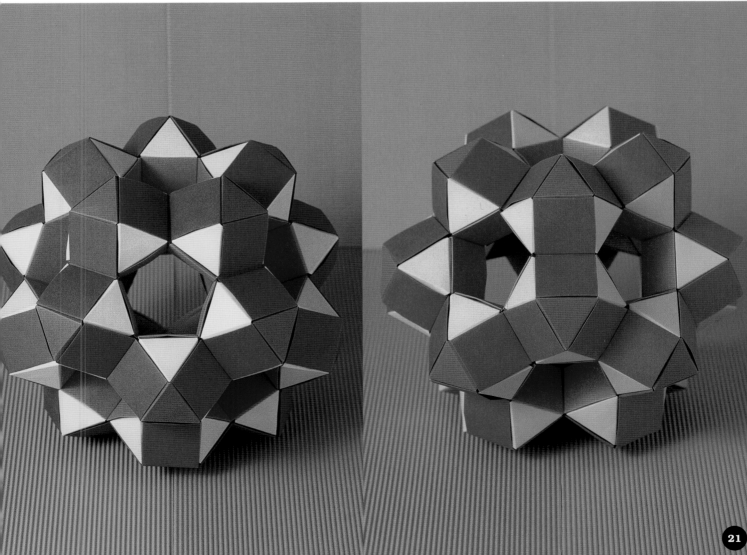

A VARIETY OF REGULAR DODECAHEDRONS

Surface patterns depend on the number of dodecahedrons used. It is possible to assemble them with 60 or 120 rhomboid units.

VARIANT KUSUDAMA DODECAHEDRON /p.30

**RHOMBIC CUBOCTAHEDRON,
DODECAHEDRON AND:
MADE WITH 120 RHOMBOID UNITS** /p.29

KUSUDAMA DODECAHEDRON /p.30

**REGULAR ICOSAHEDRON:
MADE WITH 30 RHOMBOID UNITS** /p.26

**12 REGULAR
DODECAHEDRONS** /p.24

**ICOSAHEDRON, DODECAHEDRON:
MADE WITH 60 RHOMBOID UNITS** /p.28

1

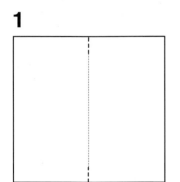

Make short creases on the upper and lower sides.

2

Fold along the line marked by the two circles to make a crease.

3

4

Make a short crease on the right side.

5

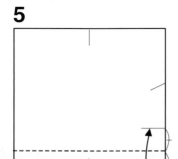

6

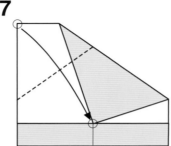

Fold so as to join the two circles ○.

7

8

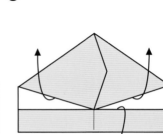

Unfold.

9

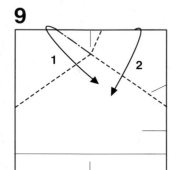

1   2

Fold in numerical order.

10

11

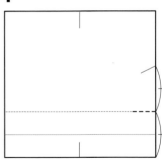

Fold so as to join the two circles ○.

12

Fold the upper corners down.

13

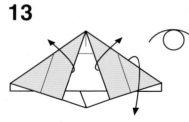

14

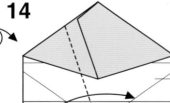

15

16

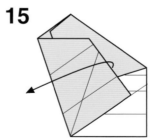

Fold the other side in the same way.

17

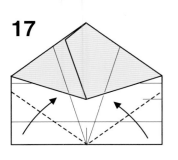

18

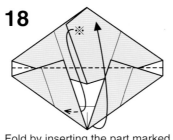

Fold by inserting the part marked with a star ※ into the pocket.

19

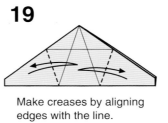

Make creases by aligning edges with the line.

20

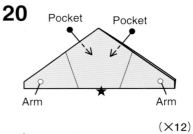

Pocket   Pocket

Arm   Arm

(×12)

★ is closed.

[Assembly Method]   Connect by joining the spots marked with stars ★.

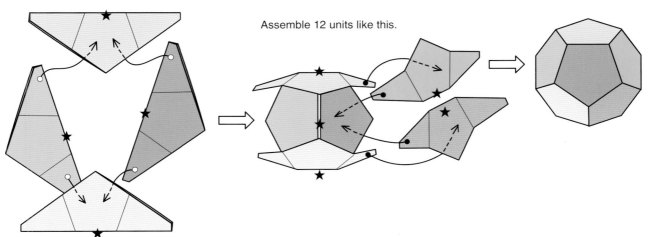

Assemble 12 units like this.

Make a rectangular pattern paper.

Methods 1-3 were worked out by Kazuo Haga.

1

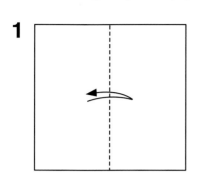

2

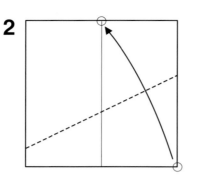

3

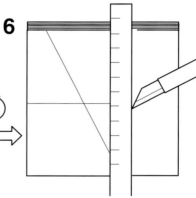

4

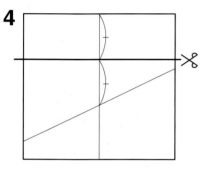

5

[Pattern paper]

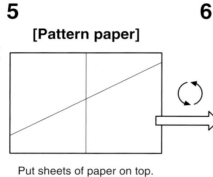

Put sheets of paper on top.

6

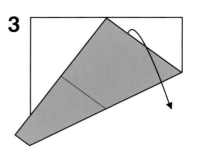

Use a cutter to cut
additional sheets
according to the
pattern.

1

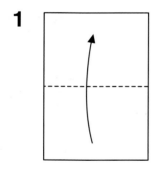

2

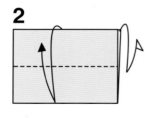

3

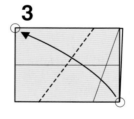

4

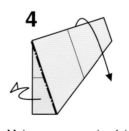

Make creases and unfold.

5

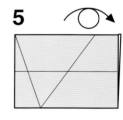

6

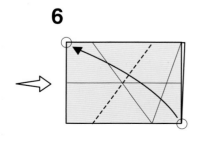

7

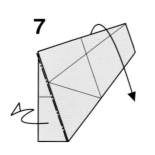

8

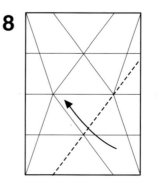

9

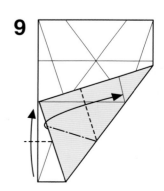

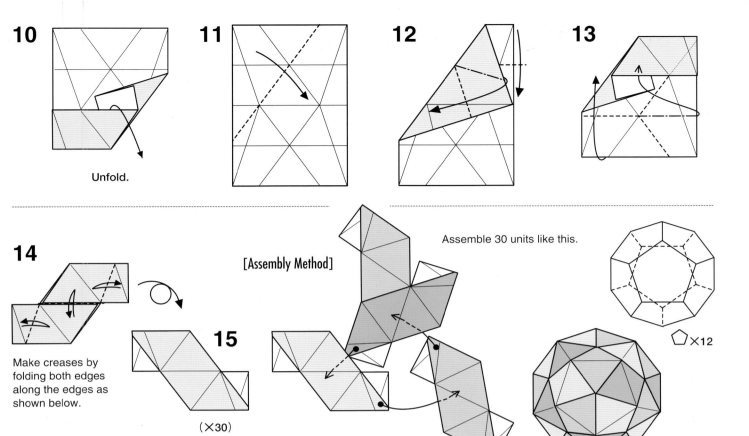

10

Unfold.

11

12

13

14

Make creases by folding both edges along the edges as shown below.

15

（×30）

[Assembly Method]

Assemble 30 units like this.

⬠ ×12

Rhomboid unit (From step 14 on p.26)

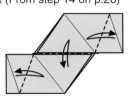 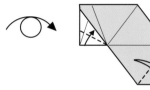 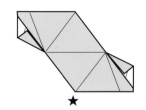

（×60）

★

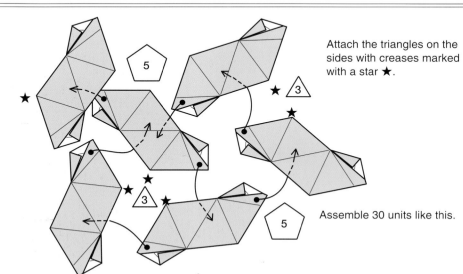

Attach the triangles on the sides with creases marked with a star ★.

★ △3

△3

Assemble 30 units like this.

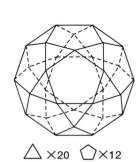

△ ×20   ⬠ ×12

Rhombic Icosa-dodecahedron STRUCTURE WITH 120 RHOMBOID UNITS | level ★★★ | 12cm×12cm

(A) has 1 crease and (B) has 2 creases. Assemble each of 60 units on the sides with the creases marked ★.

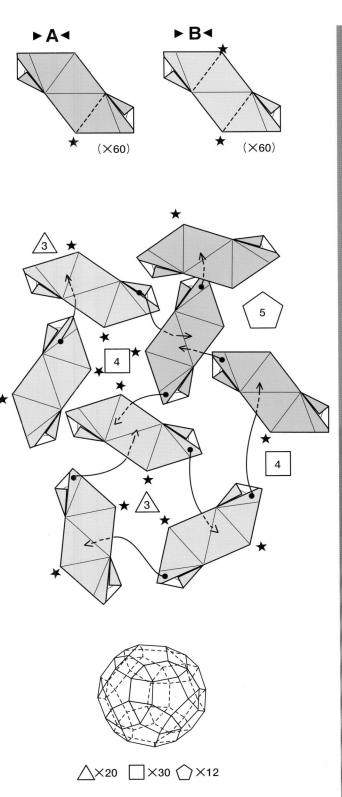

△×20 □×30 ⬠×12

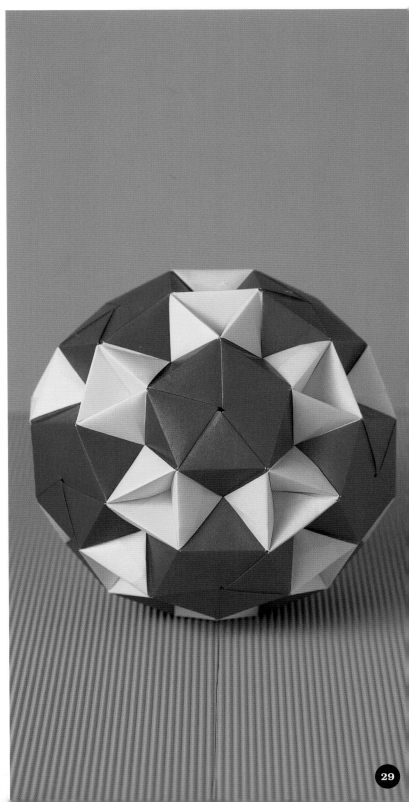

KUSUDAMA DODECAHEDRON | level ★★

Cut a square into three equal parts and make a rectangle with sides in a 1:3 ratio.

1

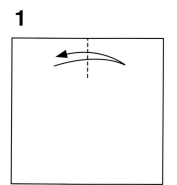

Make a short crease on
the upper side.

2

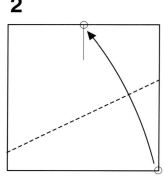

Fold so as to join the circles ○.

3

4

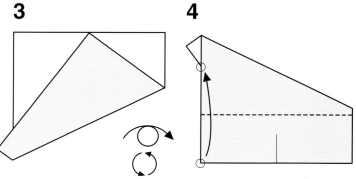

Fold so as to join the circles ○.

5

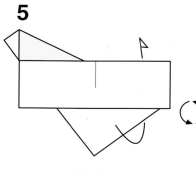

Unfold the back.

6

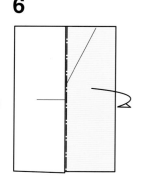

7

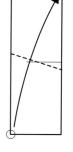

**[Use your own
judgment about where
to fold the paper]**

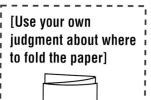

You may fold the paper into
three layers, estimating the
right place to fold it, and
then flatten it.

8

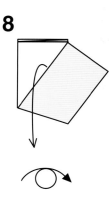

9

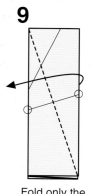

Fold only the
upper layer.

10

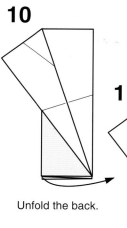

Unfold the back.

11

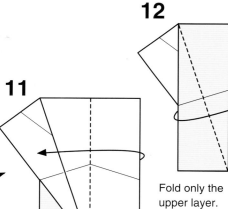

12

Fold only the
upper layer.

13

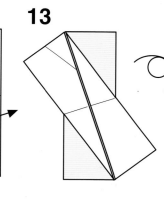

14

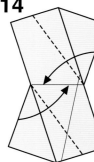

30

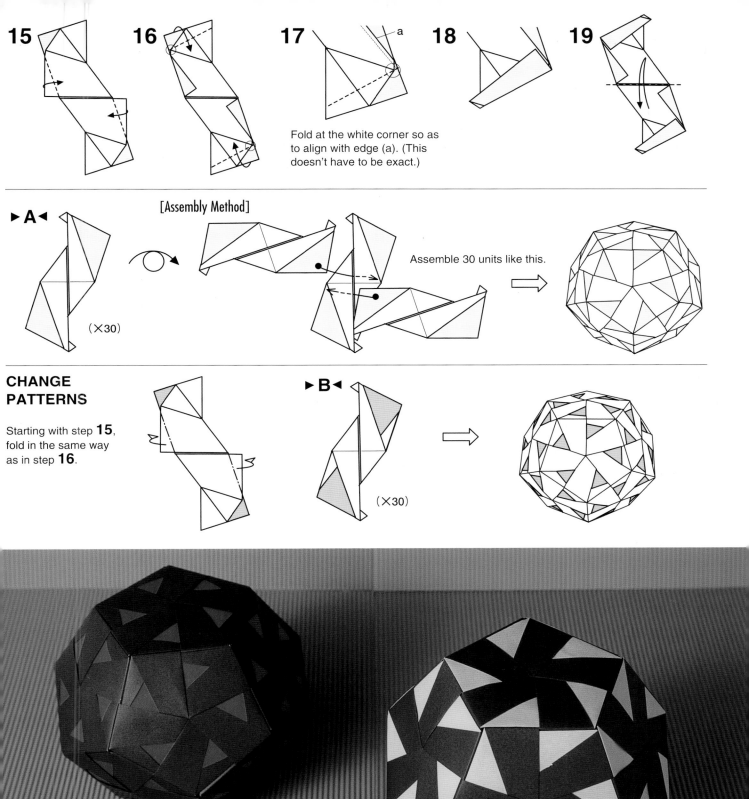

15 **16** **17**

Fold at the white corner so as to align with edge (a). (This doesn't have to be exact.)

18 **19**

►A◄

[Assembly Method]

(×30)

Assemble 30 units like this.

CHANGE PATTERNS

Starting with step **15**, fold in the same way as in step **16**.

►B◄

(×30)

4 REGULAR HEXAGONAL FLAT UNITS

There are two kinds of hexagonal flat units: one has 3 pockets on its 6 sides and the other has 6 pockets. Join the units with other elements, and create larger, more complex figures.

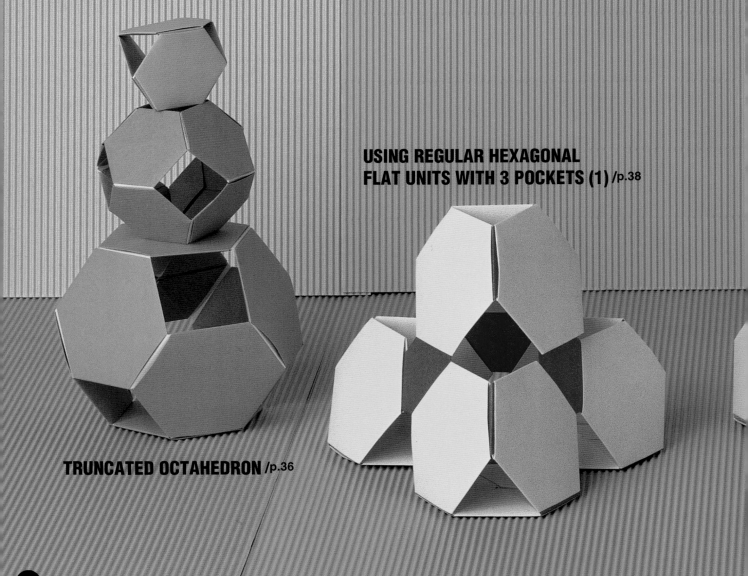

TRUNCATED TETRAHEDRON /p.36

USING REGULAR HEXAGONAL
FLAT UNITS WITH 3 POCKETS (1) /p.38

TRUNCATED OCTAHEDRON /p.36

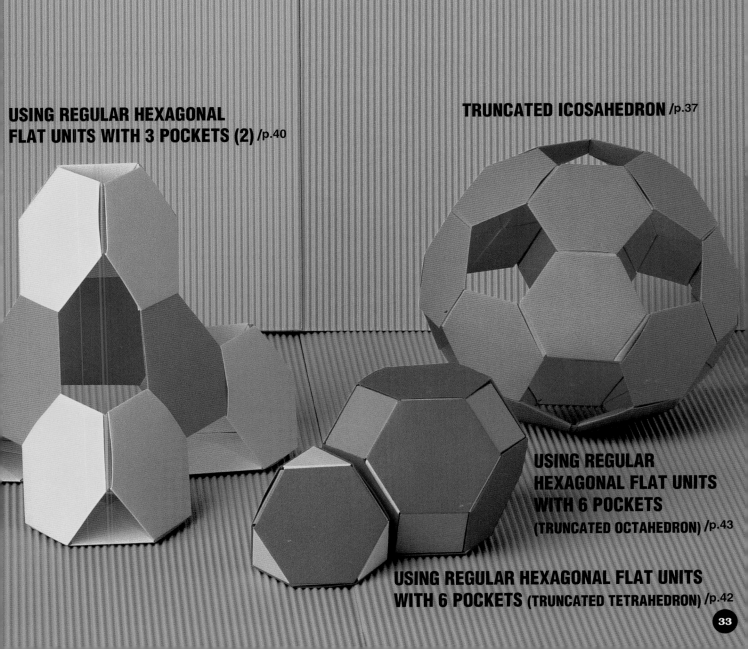

**USING REGULAR HEXAGONAL
FLAT UNITS WITH 3 POCKETS (2)** /p.40

TRUNCATED ICOSAHEDRON /p.37

**USING REGULAR
HEXAGONAL FLAT UNITS
WITH 6 POCKETS**
(TRUNCATED OCTAHEDRON) /p.43

**USING REGULAR HEXAGONAL FLAT UNITS
WITH 6 POCKETS** (TRUNCATED TETRAHEDRON) /p.42

1

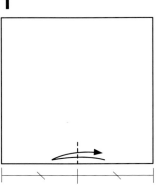

Make a short crease on the lower side.

2

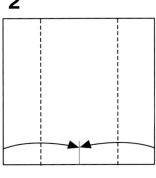

3

Fold so as to join the two circles ○, using the corner △ as the pivot.

4

5

Make a crease and unfold.

6

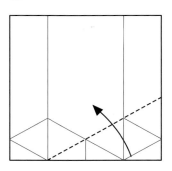

7

Leave a bit of a space between the fold and the corner.

Make a crease and unfold.

8

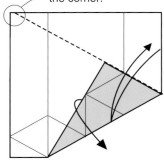

9

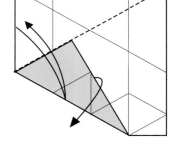

Make a crease and unfold.

10

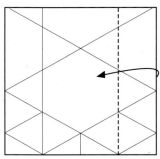

11

Fold in numerical order.

2   1

12

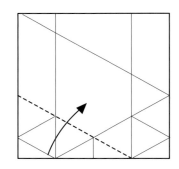

13

Fold in numerical order.

1   2

14

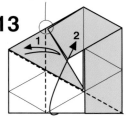

Leave a bit of a space here.

15

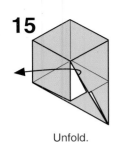

Unfold.

16

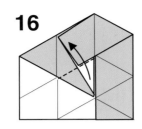

17

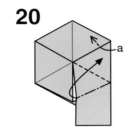

Insert flap marked with the star ☆ into the slit and fold the left side.

18

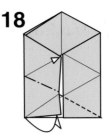

Be sure that the part marked with the triangle is securely tucked in.

Inside reverse fold

19

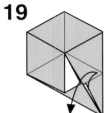

Pull out the flap.

20

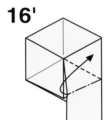

a

21

Insert the flap ★ into slit (a) of step 20.

22

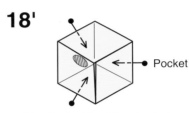

23

Pocket

Hexagonal flat unit

Simple Form

15'

Pull out the flap.

16'

17'

18'

Pocket

Glue the inside of the shaded part so that it stays in place.

Joint C

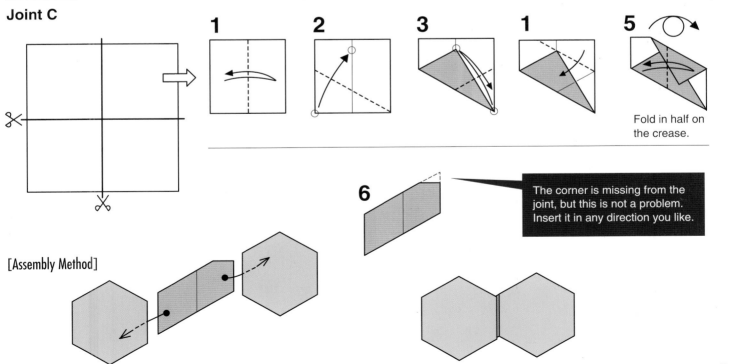

1

2

3

1

5

Fold in half on the crease.

6

The corner is missing from the joint, but this is not a problem. Insert it in any direction you like.

[Assembly Method]

Hexagonal flat unit (p. 34)　　　Joint C (p. 35)　　　　　Hexagonal flat unit (p. 34)　　　Joint C (p. 35)

(×4)　　　　　　(×6)　　　　　　　　(×8)　　　　　　(×12)

The finished work appears to have "windows."

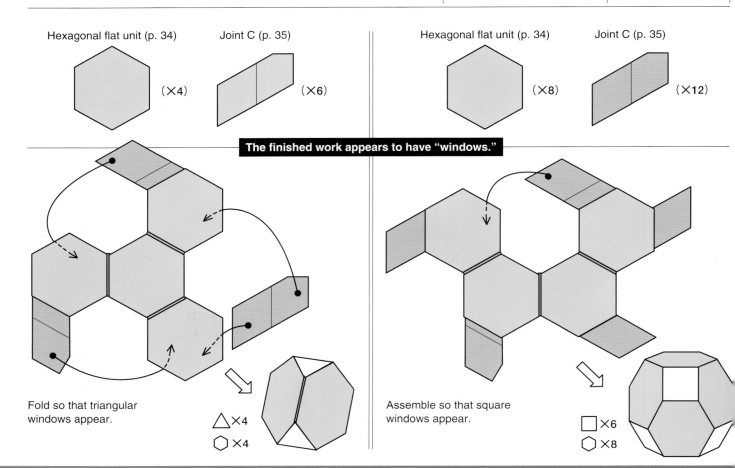

Fold so that triangular windows appear.

△×4
⬡×4

Assemble so that square windows appear.

☐×6
⬡×8

TRUNCATED ICOSAHEDRON | level ★

Hexagonal flat unit (p. 34)

(×20)

Joint C (p. 35)

(×30)

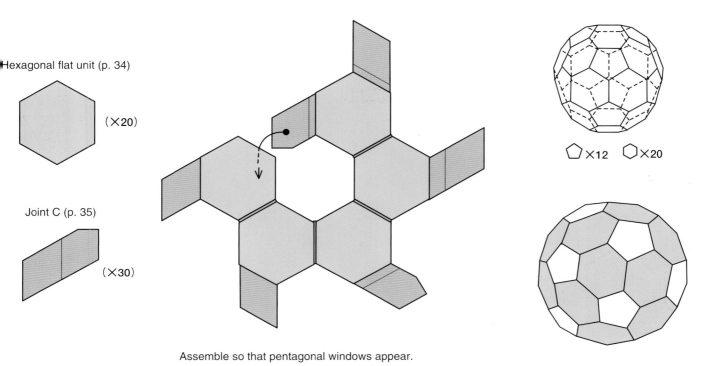

×12 ×20

Assemble so that pentagonal windows appear.

Triangle Element A

1

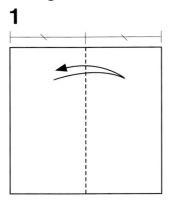

2

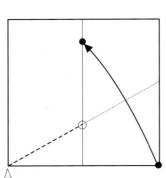

3

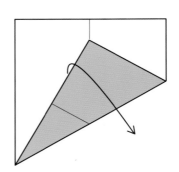

4

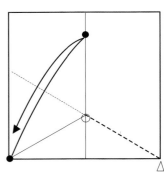

Fold the corner marked with the black dot up to the other black dot, using the corner marked with a triangle as the pivot.

5

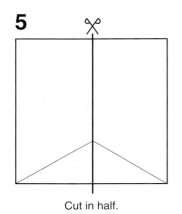

Cut in half.

6

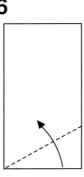

7

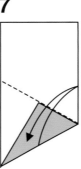

8

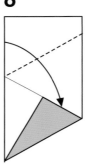

9

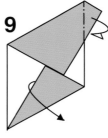

Fold under into the space between the two layers.

10

[Assembly Method]

Hexagonal flat unit (p. 34)

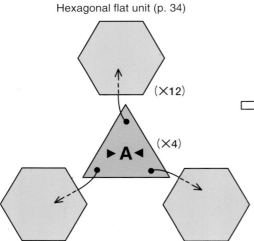

(×12)

(×4)

►**A**◄

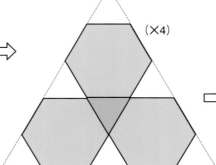

(×4)

Treat this unit as an equilateral triangle when you assemble the figure.

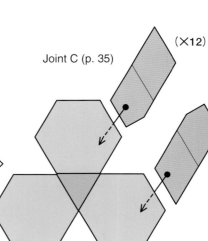

Joint C (p. 35)

(×12)

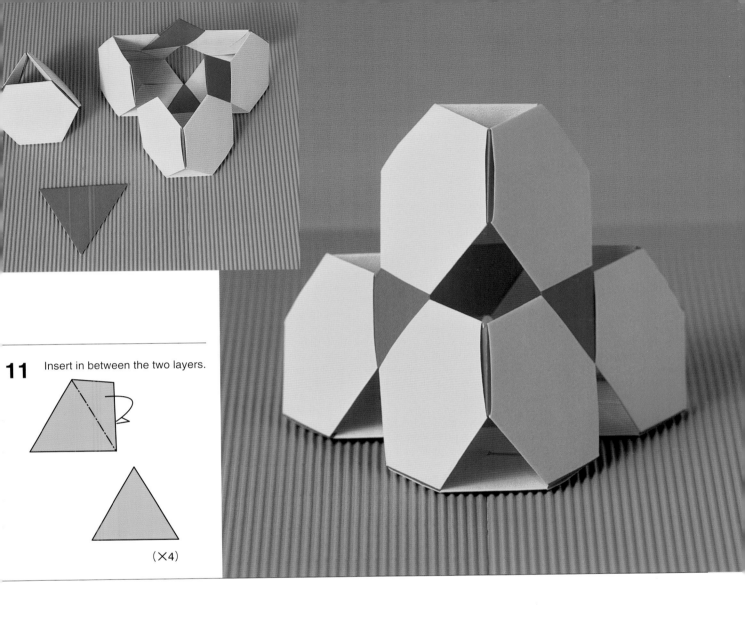

11 Insert in between the two layers.

(×4)

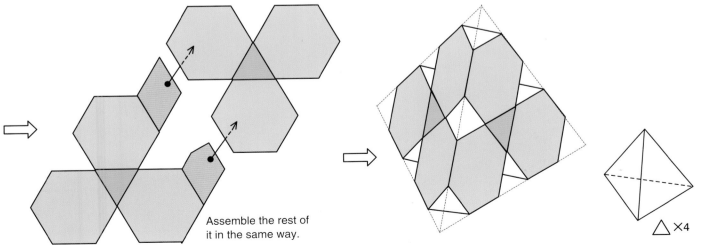

Assemble the rest of
it in the same way.

△×4

Triangle Element B

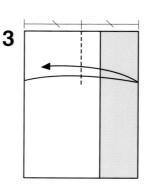

1

Make a short crease on the lower side.

2

3

4

Fold so as to join the two circles ○.

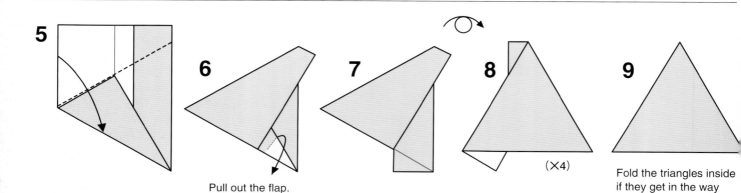

5

6

Pull out the flap.

7

8

(×4)

9

Fold the triangles inside if they get in the way during assembly.

[Assembly Method]

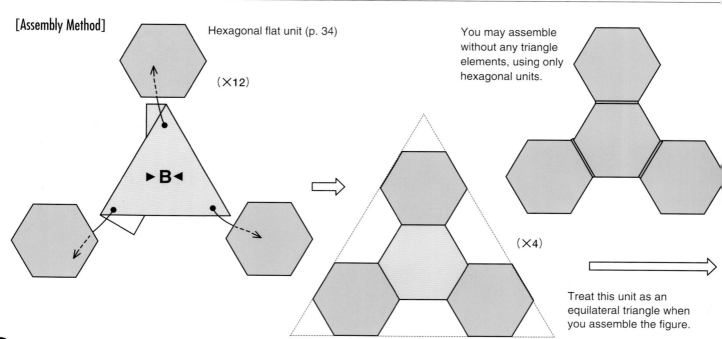

Hexagonal flat unit (p. 34)

(×12)

►**B**◄

You may assemble without any triangle elements, using only hexagonal units.

(×4)

Treat this unit as an equilateral triangle when you assemble the figure.

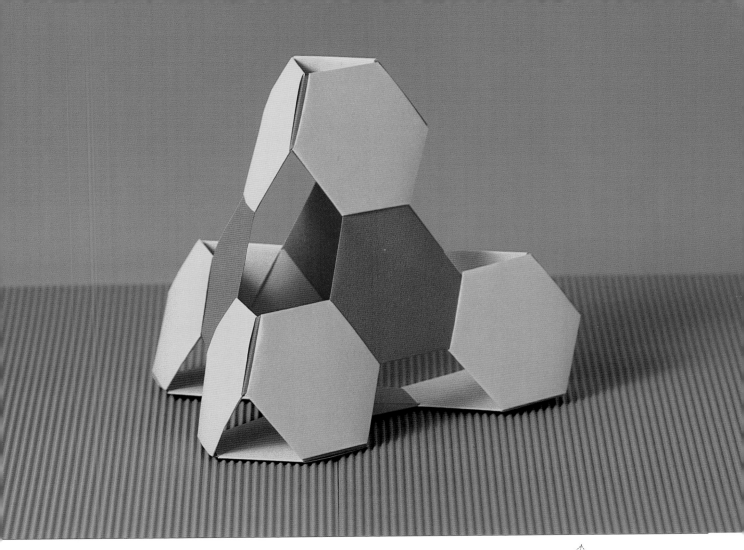

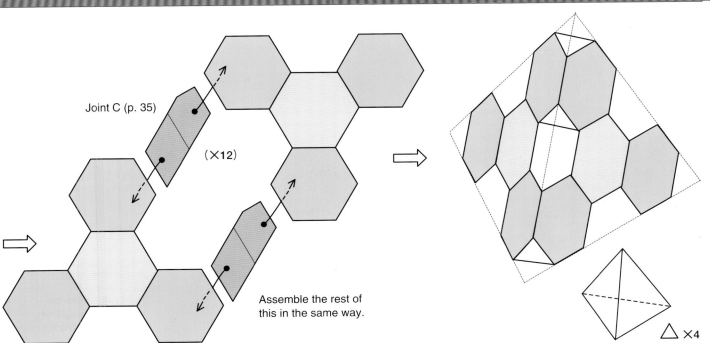

Joint C (p. 35)

(×12)

Assemble the rest of this in the same way.

△ ×4

Now you will learn to make structures with two units stacked on top of each other.
Using this unit, you can make the solids shown on pp. 38-41 without windows. You can also use it on p. 36.

Hexagonal Flat Unit (Simple Form) (Starting from step 16' on p. 35)

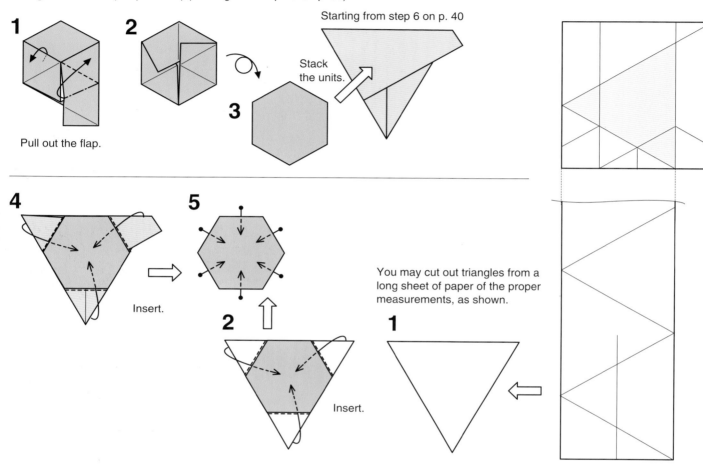

1 Pull out the flap.

2

3 Stack the units.

Starting from step 6 on p. 40

4 Insert.

5

2 Insert.

1

You may cut out triangles from a long sheet of paper of the proper measurements, as shown.

Triangle Element C

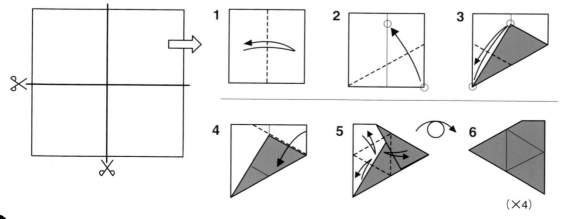

1

2

3

4

5

6

(×4)

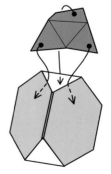

Make a truncated tetrahedron (see p.36) and insert the elements into the triangle windows.

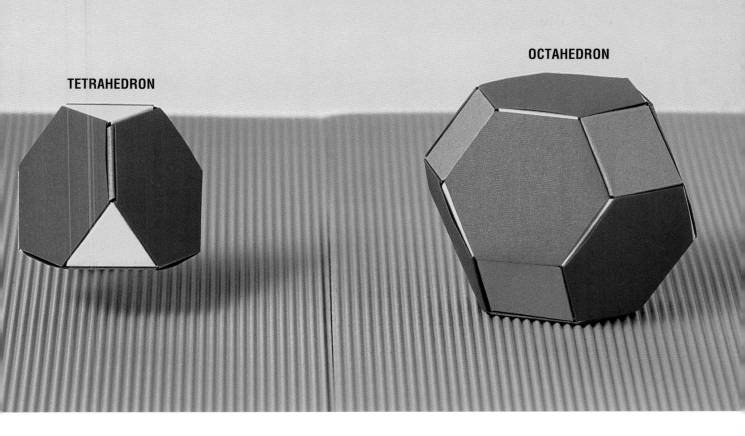

TETRAHEDRON

OCTAHEDRON

Square Element

1

2

3

4

4 Make a crease
and unfold.

5

6

7

8

(×6)

Make a truncated octahedron (see
p. 36) and insert the elements into
the square windows.

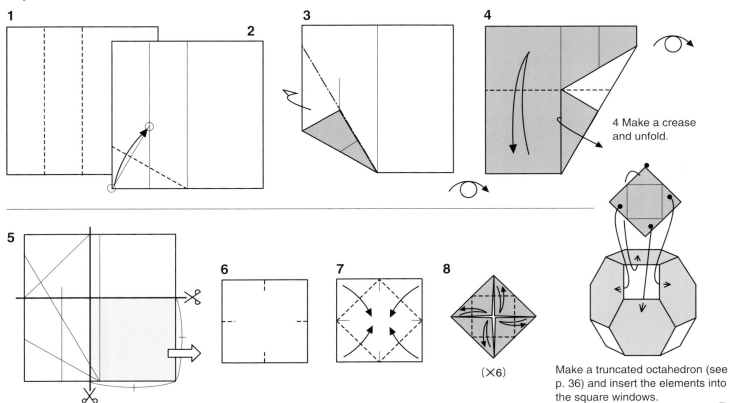

43

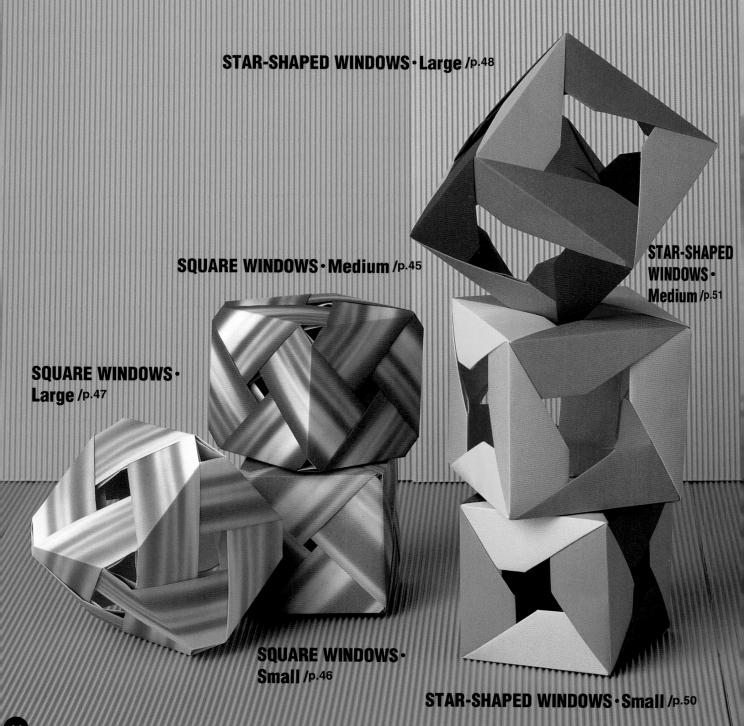

5 | EDGE CUBES

These cubes are assembled by connecting them at twelve places. There are square or star-shaped windows in the middle of each surface. Modifying the folds and measurements changes the cubes and the size of the windows.

STAR-SHAPED WINDOWS·Large /p.48

STAR-SHAPED WINDOWS· Medium/p.51

SQUARE WINDOWS·Medium /p.45

SQUARE WINDOWS· Large /p.47

SQUARE WINDOWS· Small /p.46

STAR-SHAPED WINDOWS·Small /p.50

This cube is assembled by joining the sides. Changing the folds and the measurements changes the size of the windows.

1

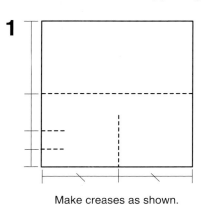

Make creases as shown.

2

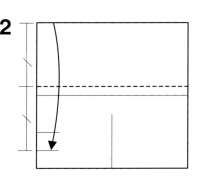

3

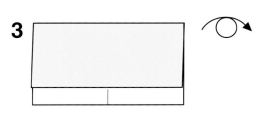

4

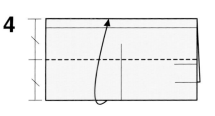

Align the edges and fold.

5

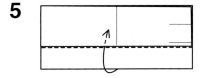

Fold the edge under the flap.

6

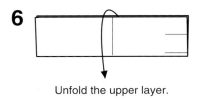

Unfold the upper layer.

7

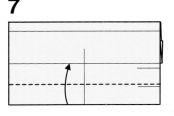

8

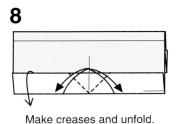

Make creases and unfold.

9

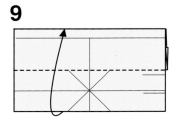

10

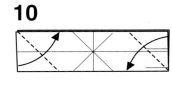

11

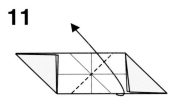

12

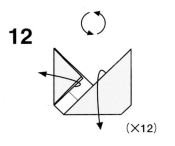

(×12)

[Assembly Method]

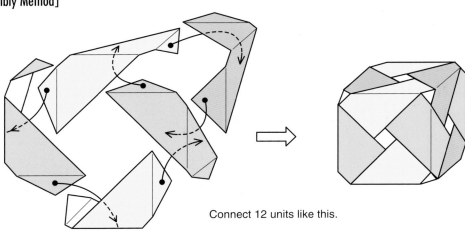

Connect 12 units like this.

45

A cube assembled by connecting sides. Changing the folds and the measurements changes the size of the windows.

1

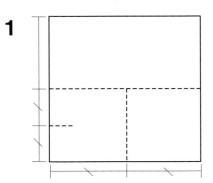

Make creases as shown.

2

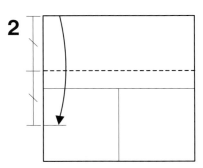

3

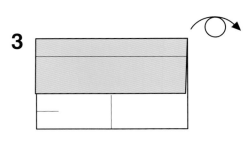

4

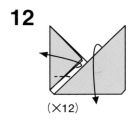

Align edges and fold.

5

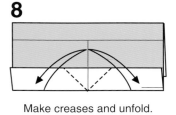

Fold under the flap.

6

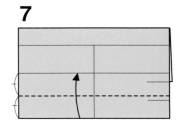

Unfold the upper layer.

7

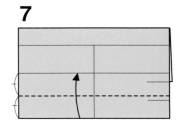

8

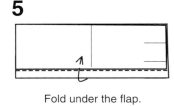

Make creases and unfold.

9

10

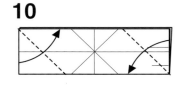

11

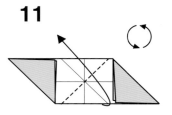

12

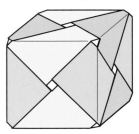

(×12)

Assemble in the same way as the medium cube. (p. 45)

Edge Cube SQUARE WINDOWS · Large | level ★★ | 15cm × 15cm

1

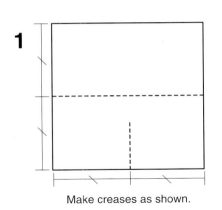

Make creases as shown.

2

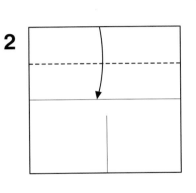

3

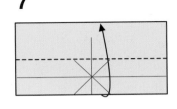

4

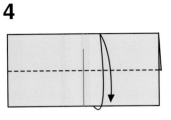

Align the edges and fold.

5

6

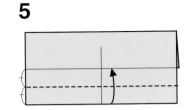

Make creases and unfold.

7

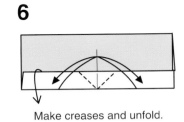

8

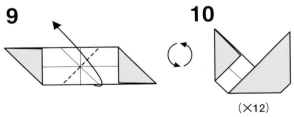

9

10

（×12）

Assemble in the same way as the medium cube. (p. 45)

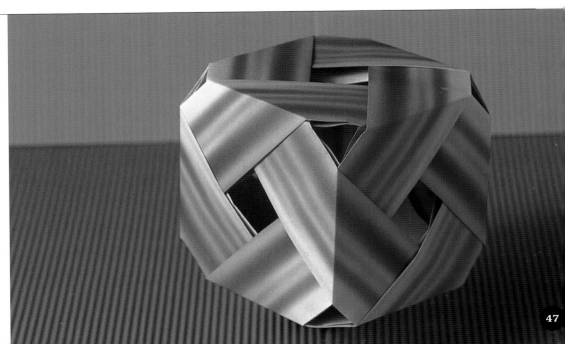

A cube with star-shaped windows. Changing the folds and the measurements changes the size of the windows.

1

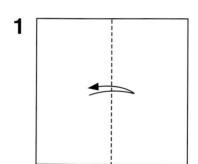

2

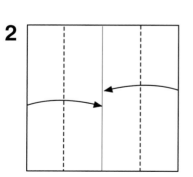

3

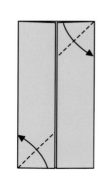

4

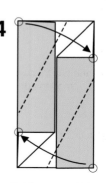

Fold so as to join
the two circles ◯.

5

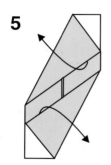

Unfold.

6

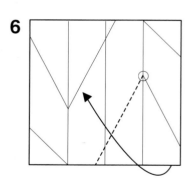

Fold to the place indicated
by the circle ◯.

7

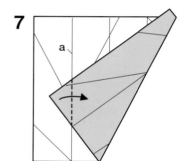

a

Fold on line (a).

8

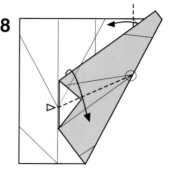

Fold on line between the
triangle △ and the circle ◯.

9

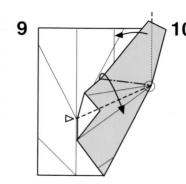

Intermediate form.

10

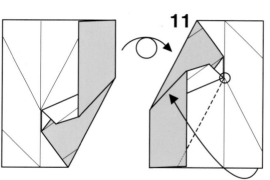

Fold to the place indicated
by the circle ◯.

11

Fold the triangle
along the side.

12

13

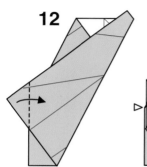
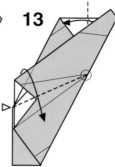

Fold a crease
between the triangle
△ and the circle ◯.

14

Tuck the tab marked with a star ★ inside the folds.

15

Fold the corner inward.

16

17

18

Unfold.

19

(×12)

[Assembly Method]

Assemble 12 units like this.

From step 4 on p. 48

1
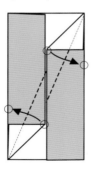

2
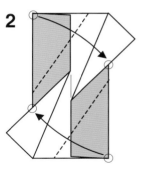

Fold so as to join the
two circles ○.

3
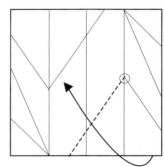

Unfold.

4

Fold to the place indicated
by the circle ○.

5
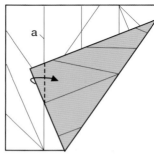

Fold on line (a).

6
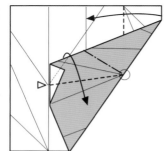

Fold on line between the
triangle △ and the circle ○.

7
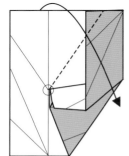

8
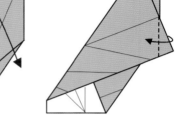

9
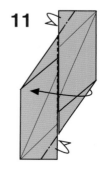

10
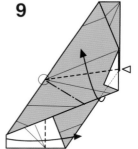

11
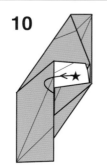

Tuck the tab marked with
a star ★ inside the folds.

12

13

Make creases
and unfold.

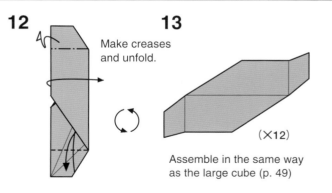

(×12)

Assemble in the same way
as the large cube (p. 49)

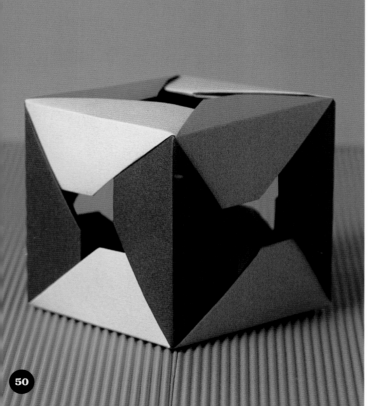

Starting from step 3 on p. 48.

1
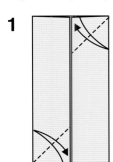

2
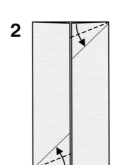

3
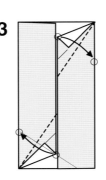

4
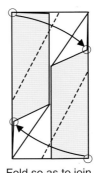

Fold so as to join the two circles ○.

5
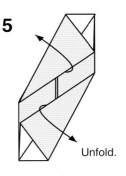

Unfold.

6
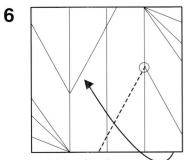

Fold to the place indicated by the circle ○.

7
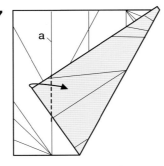

Fold on line (a).

8
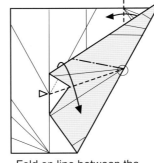

Fold on line between the triangle △ and the circle ○.

9
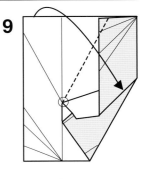

10
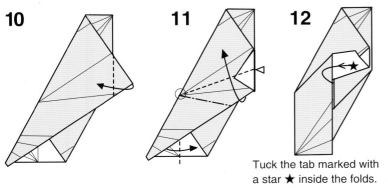

11

12

Tuck the tab marked with a star ★ inside the folds.

13
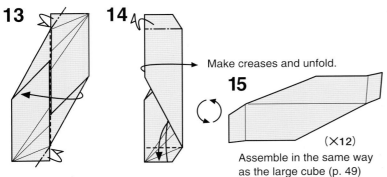

14

Make creases and unfold.

15

(✕12)

Assemble in the same way as the large cube (p. 49)

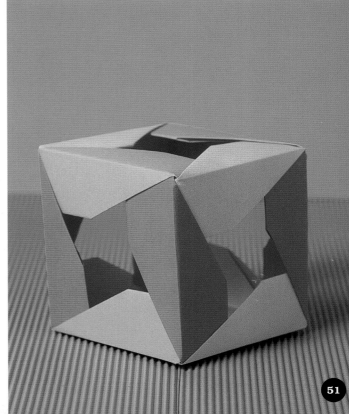

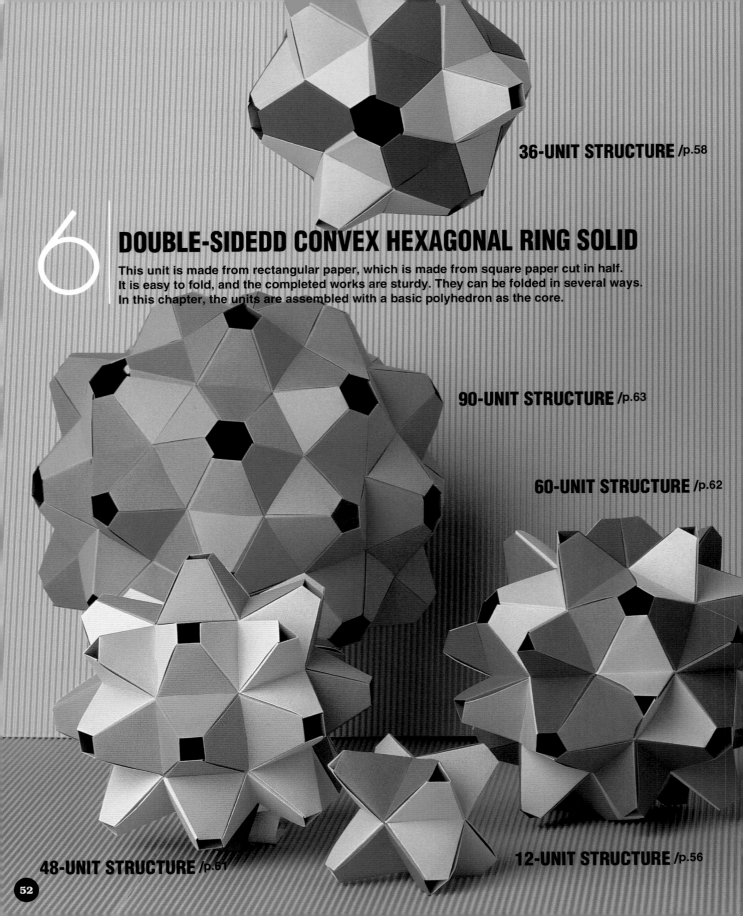

36-UNIT STRUCTURE /p.58

6 | DOUBLE-SIDEDD CONVEX HEXAGONAL RING SOLID

This unit is made from rectangular paper, which is made from square paper cut in half.
It is easy to fold, and the completed works are sturdy. They can be folded in several ways.
In this chapter, the units are assembled with a basic polyhedron as the core.

90-UNIT STRUCTURE /p.63

60-UNIT STRUCTURE /p.62

48-UNIT STRUCTURE /p.61

12-UNIT STRUCTURE /p.56

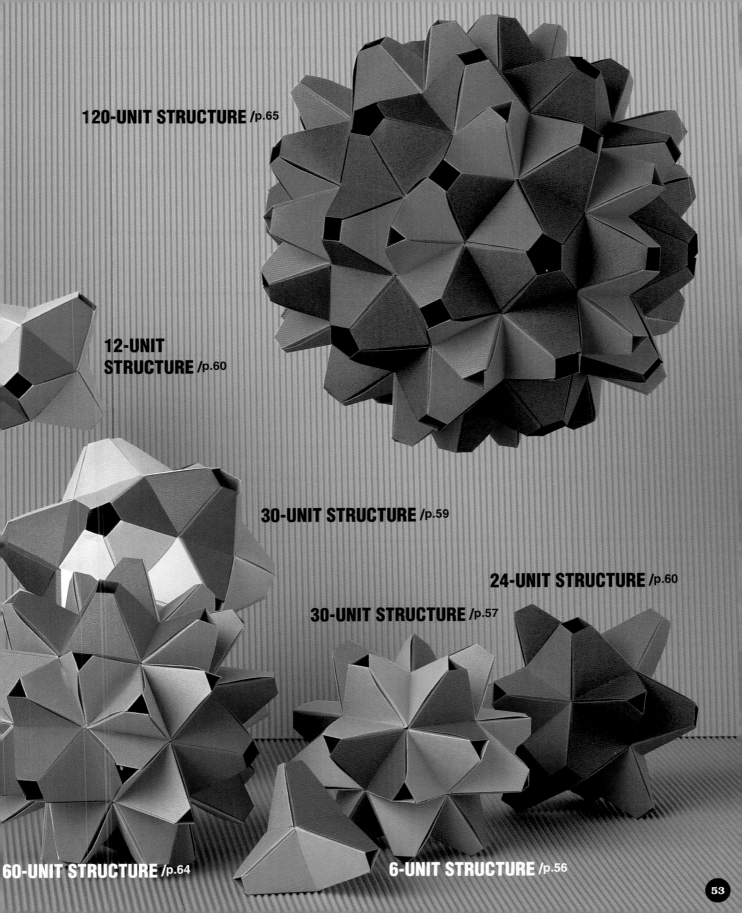

120-UNIT STRUCTURE /p.65

12-UNIT STRUCTURE /p.60

30-UNIT STRUCTURE /p.59

24-UNIT STRUCTURE /p.60

30-UNIT STRUCTURE /p.57

60-UNIT STRUCTURE /p.64

6-UNIT STRUCTURE /p.56

You can assemble this unit, using both sides of the paper. Almost all the units are sturdy, and no glue is necessary. First, let's begin with a convex style.

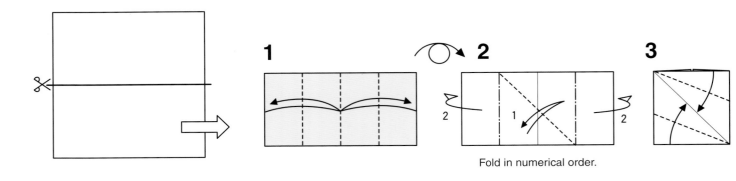

1

2

3

Fold in numerical order.

4

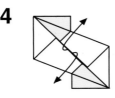

Open completely.

5

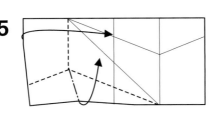

Make an inside reverse fold.

6

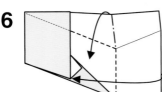

7

8

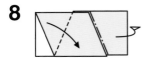

9

After creasing the paper, unfold.

10

Pocket

Completed Unit

HINT ON ASSEMBLY ①

Insert into the pocket on the side. Disregard the slit in the middle of the unit since it is used as a fold. Notice especially the small triangle (shaded) folded in step 9. This triangle hooks onto the joint and make the assembly sturdy.

1

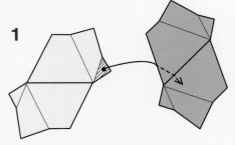

Insert the shaded triangle fully over the ridge of the other unit.

2

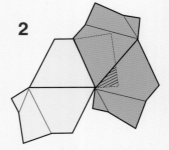

Insert the triangle like this.

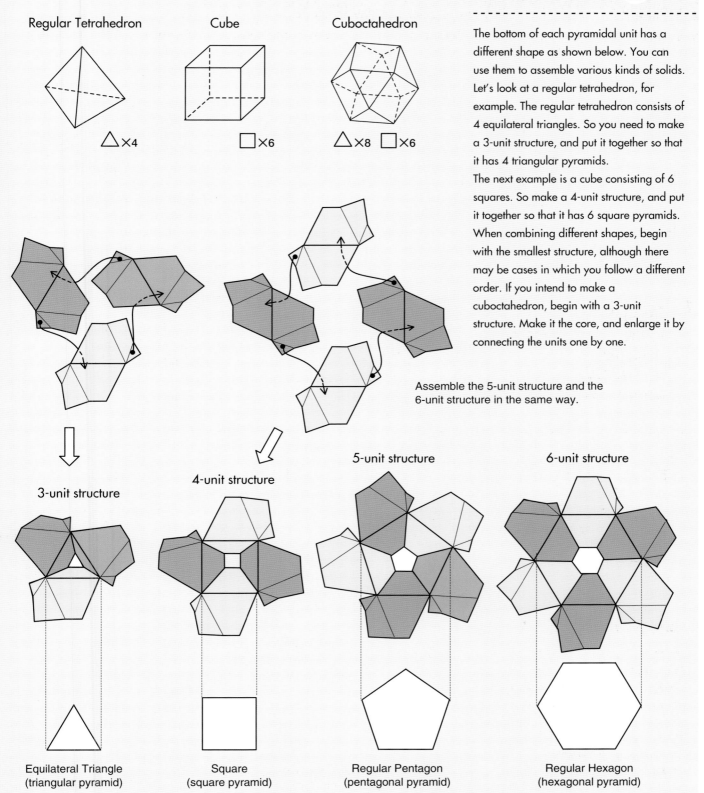

Regular Tetrahedron

△×4

Cube

□×6

Cuboctahedron

△×8 □×6

The bottom of each pyramidal unit has a different shape as shown below. You can use them to assemble various kinds of solids. Let's look at a regular tetrahedron, for example. The regular tetrahedron consists of 4 equilateral triangles. So you need to make a 3-unit structure, and put it together so that it has 4 triangular pyramids.

The next example is a cube consisting of 6 squares. So make a 4-unit structure, and put it together so that it has 6 square pyramids.

When combining different shapes, begin with the smallest structure, although there may be cases in which you follow a different order. If you intend to make a cuboctahedron, begin with a 3-unit structure. Make it the core, and enlarge it by connecting the units one by one.

Assemble the 5-unit structure and the 6-unit structure in the same way.

3-unit structure

4-unit structure

5-unit structure

6-unit structure

Equilateral Triangle
(triangular pyramid)

Square
(square pyramid)

Regular Pentagon
(pentagonal pyramid)

Regular Hexagon
(hexagonal pyramid)

6-UNIT STRUCTURE Regular Tetrahedron, 12-UNIT STRUCTURE Octahedron | level ★ | 12cm×6cm

Double-sidedd convex hexagonal ring (p. 54)

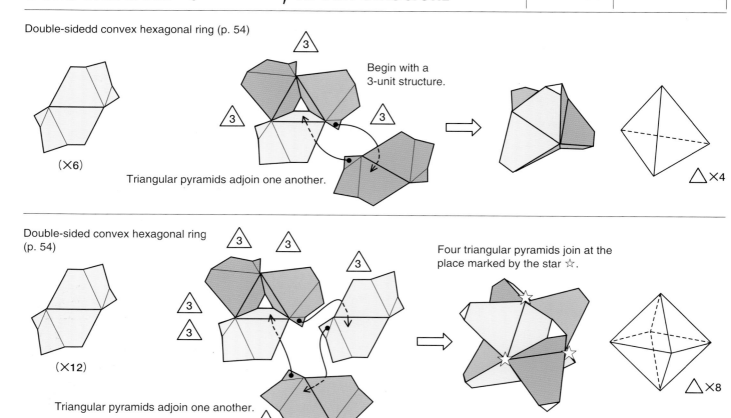

(×6)

Triangular pyramids adjoin one another.

Begin with a 3-unit structure.

△×4

Double-sided convex hexagonal ring (p. 54)

(×12)

Triangular pyramids adjoin one another.

Four triangular pyramids join at the place marked by the star ☆.

△×8

30-UNIT STRUCTURE Regular Icosahedron | level ★★

Double-sided convex hexagonal ring (p. 54)

Make 5 triangular pyramids centered around the place marked with a star ☆.

Five triangular pyramids join at the place marked with a star ☆.

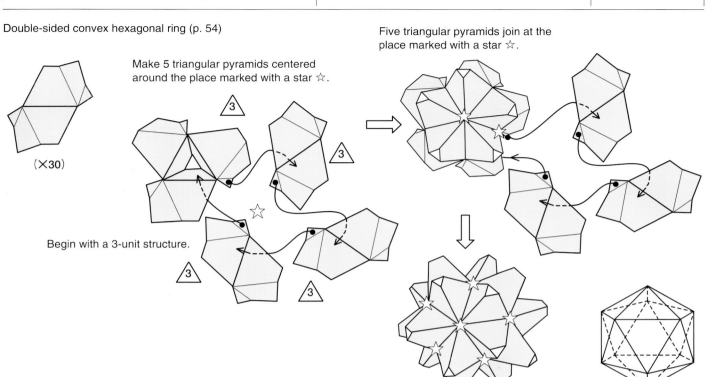

(×30)

Begin with a 3-unit structure.

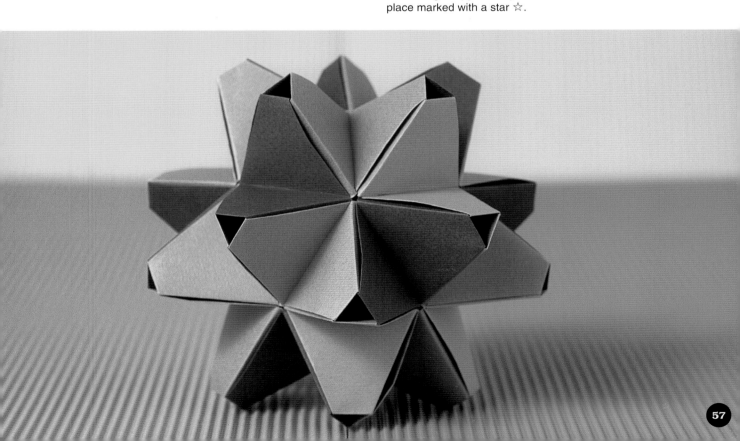

Five triangular pyramids join at the place marked with a star ☆.

△×20

Double-sided convex hexagonal ring (p. 54)

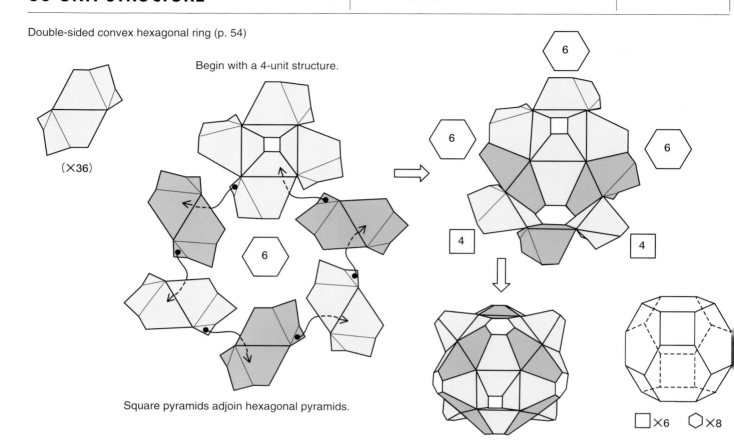

Begin with a 4-unit structure.

(×36)

6

6

6

6

4   4

Square pyramids adjoin hexagonal pyramids.

□×6   ⬡×8

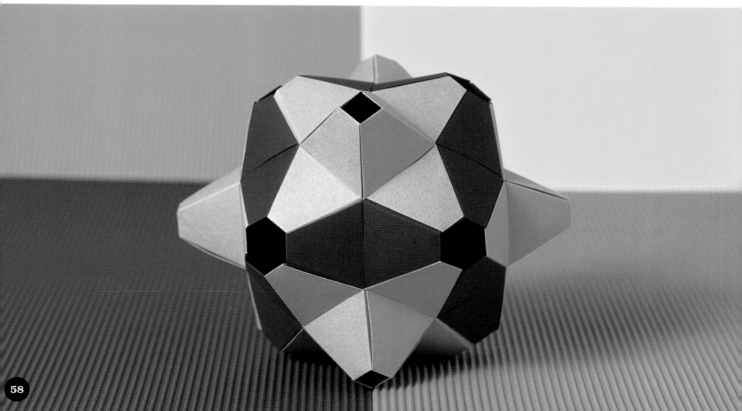

58

30-UNIT STRUCTURE Regular Dodecahedron | level ★ | 12cm × 6cm

Double-sided convex hexagonal ring (p. 54)

(×30)

Begin with a
5-unit structure.

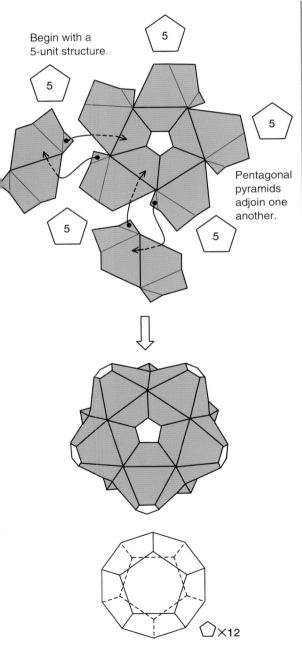

5

5

5

5

5

Pentagonal
pyramids
adjoin one
another.

×12

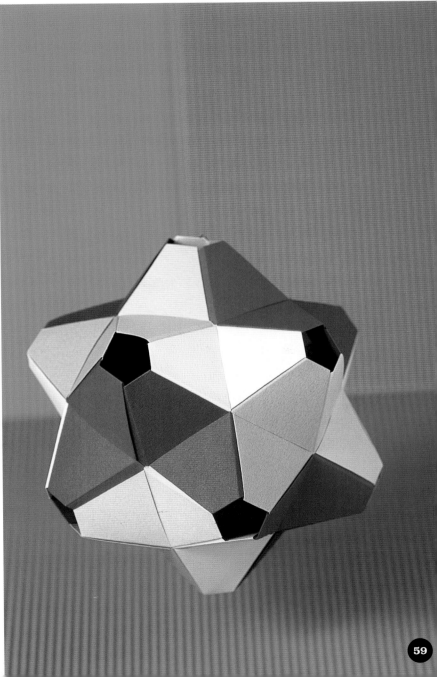

12-UNIT STRUCTURE Cube, 24-UNIT STRUCTURE Cuboctahedron | level ★ | 12cm×6cm

Double-sided convex hexagonal ring (p. 54)

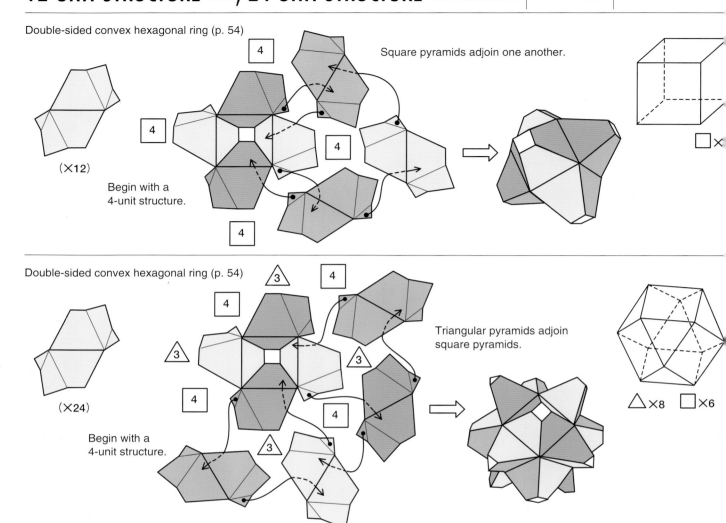

Square pyramids adjoin one another.

(×12)

Begin with a 4-unit structure.

4 4 4 4

□×

Double-sided convex hexagonal ring (p. 54)

(×24)

Begin with a 4-unit structure.

Triangular pyramids adjoin square pyramids.

3 4 4 3 4 3 3

△×8 □×6

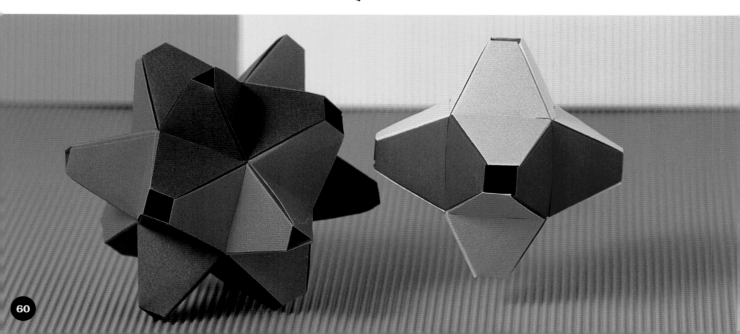

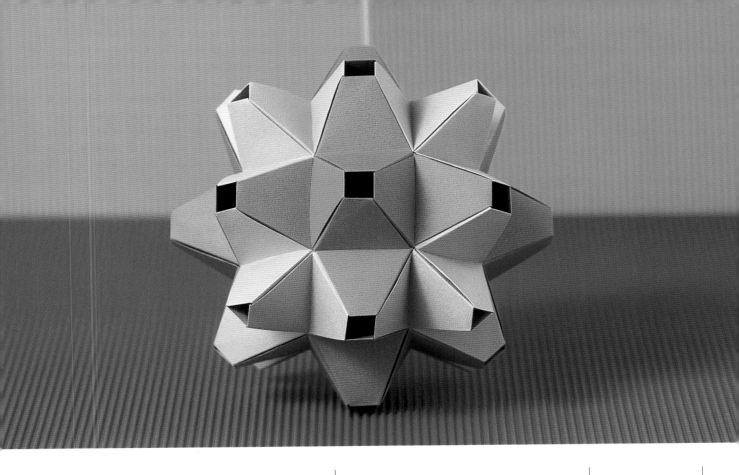

48-UNIT STRUCTURE Rhombic Cuboctahedron | **level** ★★

$12cm \times 6cm$

Double-sided convex hexagonal ring (p. 54)

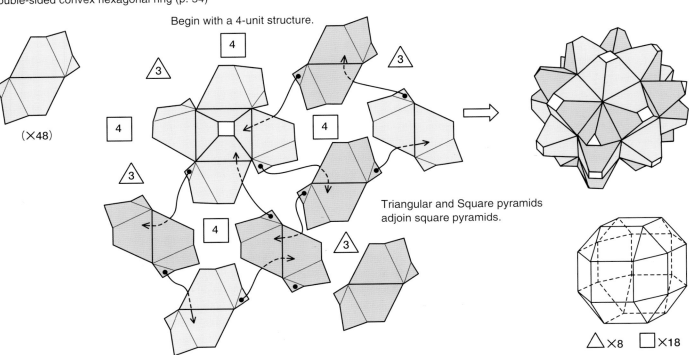

Begin with a 4-unit structure.

(×48)

Triangular and Square pyramids adjoin square pyramids.

△×8   □×18

60-UNIT STRUCTURE Icosahedron/Dodecahedron | level ★★

Double-sided convex hexagonal ring (p. 54)

Begin with a 5-unit structure.

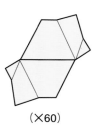

(×60)

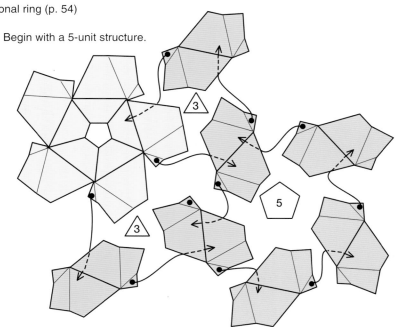

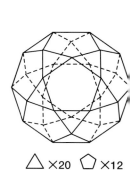

Triangular pyramids adjoin pentagonal pyramids.

△ ×20 ⬠ ×12

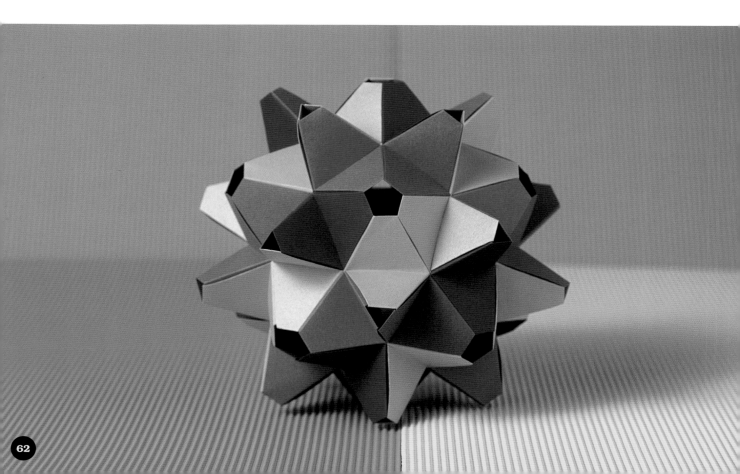

Double-sided convex hexagonal ring (p. 54)

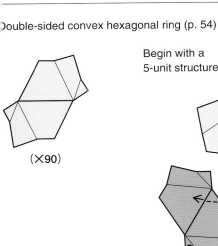

(✕90)

Begin with a
5-unit structure.

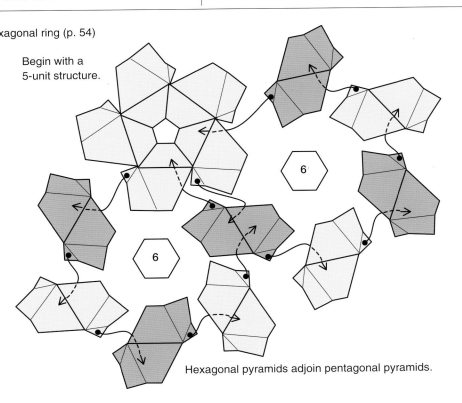

6

6

Hexagonal pyramids adjoin pentagonal pyramids.

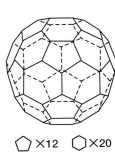

⬠ ✕12 ⬡ ✕20

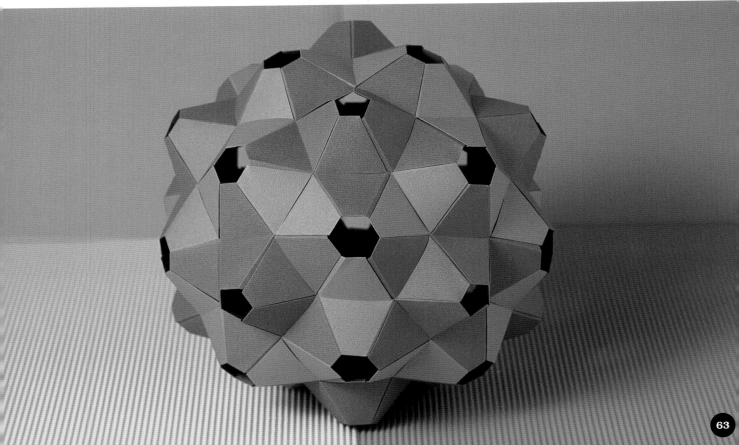

60-UNIT STRUCTURE Variant Cube | level ★★ | 12cm×6cm

Double-sided convex hexagonal ring (p. 54)

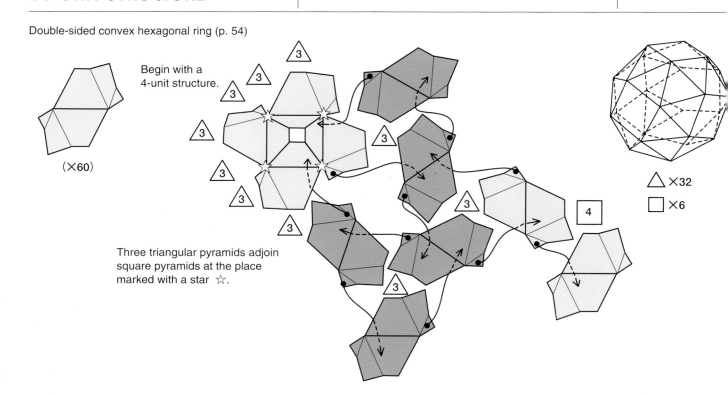

Begin with a 4-unit structure.

(×60)

Three triangular pyramids adjoin square pyramids at the place marked with a star ☆.

△ ×32

□ ×6

Double-sided convex hexagonal ring (p. 54)

（×120）

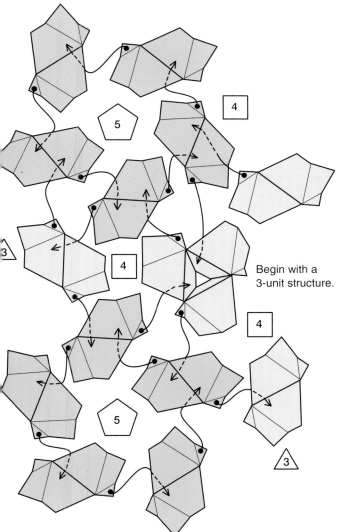

5

4

3

4

Begin with a
3-unit structure.

4

5

3

The sides that adjoin the pentagon are square.
The sides that adjoin the triangle are square.

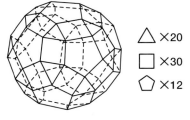

△ ×20
□ ×30
⬠ ×12

7 | DOUBLE-SIDED CONCAVE HEXAGONAL RING SOLIDS

This is the inverse of a double-sided convex hexagonal ring. The core polyhedrons are the same, but convex structures and concave structures give a different visual impression.
It's interesting to set the two finished works next to each other.

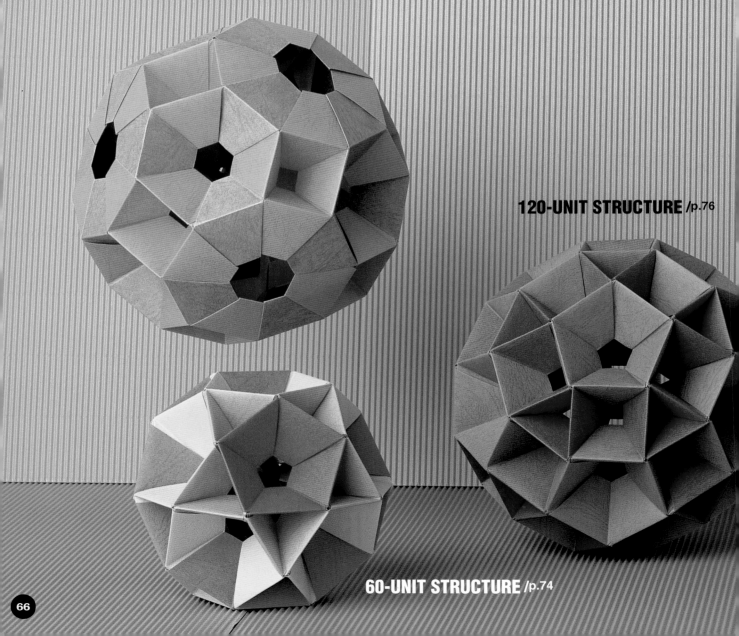

72-UNIT STRUCTURE /p.73

120-UNIT STRUCTURE /p.76

60-UNIT STRUCTURE /p.74

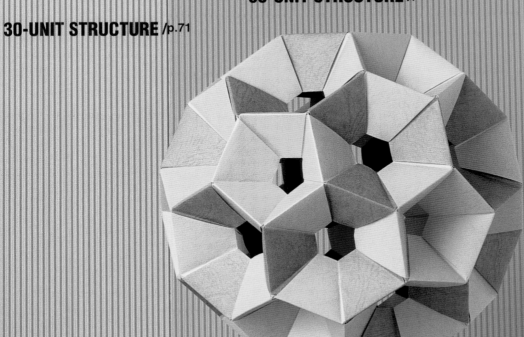

30-UNIT STRUCTURE /p.71

90-UNIT STRUCTURE /p.75

36-UNIT STRUCTURE /p.72

36-UNIT STRUCTURE /p.70

DOUBLE-SIDED CONCAVE HEXAGONAL RING SOLID

level ★ 12cm✕16cm

The structure is the same as that of the double-sided convex hexagonal ring solid. However, you use a different folding method when assembling it in order to hide the extra lines. The finished works are sturdy, so glue is not necessary. Unit B, which is used in some structures, has a crease only on one side.

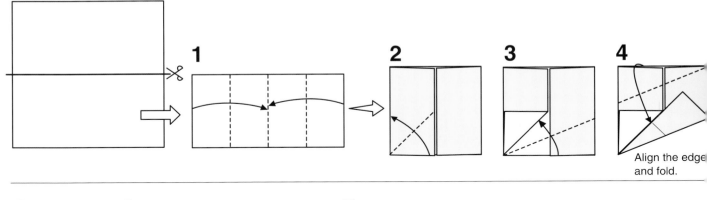

1

2

3

4

Align the edge and fold.

5
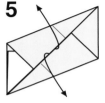
Open completely.

6
Make an inside reverse fold.

7
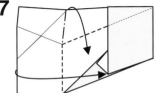

8
Fold in half.

9
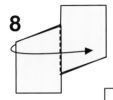

10

After creasing, unfold.

11 A
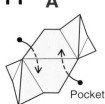
Pocket

9

Make a crease on one side.

10'

After creasing, unfold.

11' B

C
Creased step 1

HINT ON ASSEMBLY 1

Take special note of the small triangle (shaded) in step 10. This triangle hooks firmly and makes the unit sturdy.

1

Insert the shaded triangle fully over the ridge of the other unit.

2

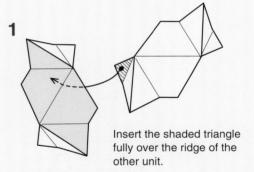

Insert the triangle like this.

HINT ON ASSEMBLY 2

As is seen in the figures, the units are indented along the ridges. You can assemble various kinds of solids by making use of them.
One example is a truncated octahedron. It consists of squares and hexagons.

First, make 4-unit structures and put them together so that the hexagons are connected adjoin around the square indentation.
Begin with the smallest structure (a 4-unit structure in this case). Make it the core, and expand it by connecting additional units one by one.

Truncated Octahedron

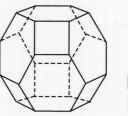

☐ ×6
⬡ ×8

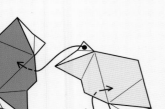

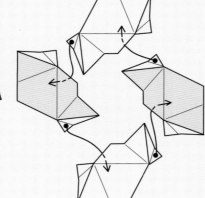

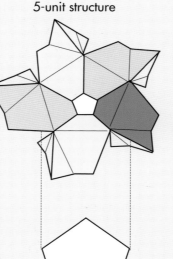

Assemble 5-unit and 6-unit structures in the same fashion.

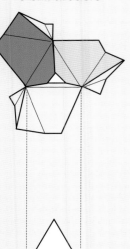

3-unit structure

4-unit structure

5-unit structure

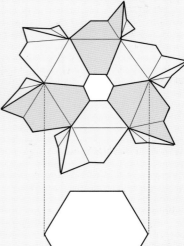

6-unit structure

Equilateral Triangle
(Triangular indentation)

Square
(Square indentation)

Regular Pentagon
(Pentagonal indentation)

Regular Hexagon
(Hexagonal indentation)

36-UNIT STRUCTURE Truncated Hexahedron | level ★★

Double-sided concave hexagonal ring (p.68)

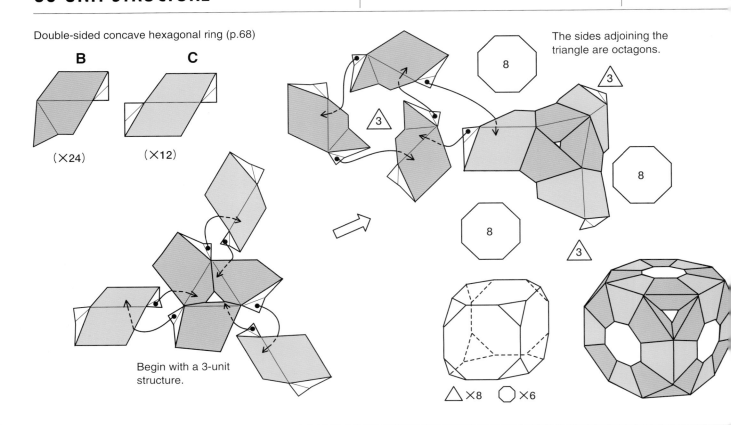

B (×24)

C (×12)

Begin with a 3-unit structure.

The sides adjoining the triangle are octagons.

8
3
8
8
3

△×8 ⬡×6

ouble-sided concave hexagonal ring (p.68)

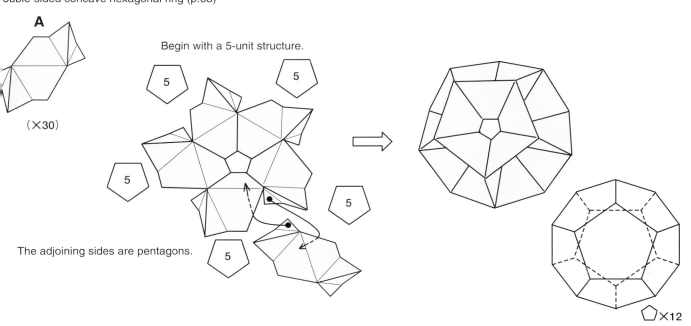

A

(×30)

Begin with a 5-unit structure.

The adjoining sides are pentagons.

5   5   5   5   5

×12

36-UNIT STRUCTURE Truncated Octahedron | level ★★

Double-sided concave hexagonal ring (p.68)

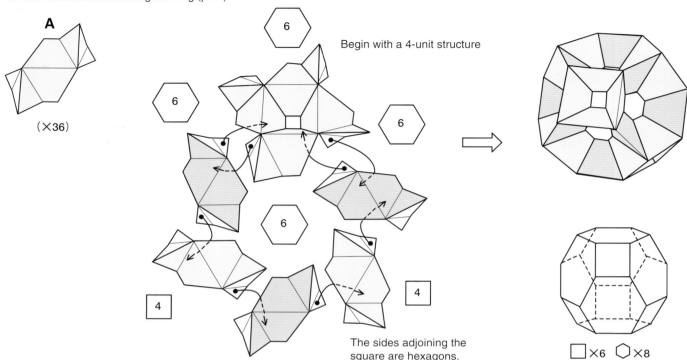

A

（×36）

6

6

Begin with a 4-unit structure

6

6

4

4

The sides adjoining the
square are hexagons.

☐×6 ⬡×8

Double-sided concave hexagonal ring (p.68)

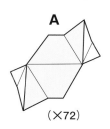

A

（×72）

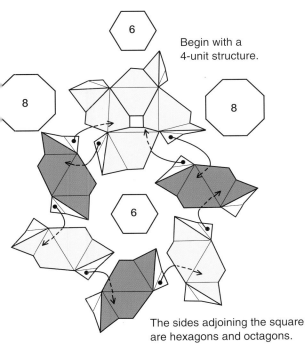

6

Begin with a
4-unit structure.

8

8

6

The sides adjoining the square
are hexagons and octagons.

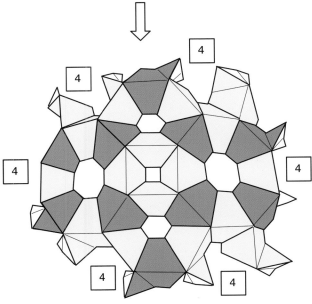

4

4

4

4

4

4

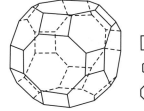

☐ ×12

⬡ ×8

⬣ ×6

73

60-UNIT STRUCTURE Icosahedron/Dodecahedron | level ★★ | 12cm×6cm

Double-sided concave hexagonal ring (p.68)

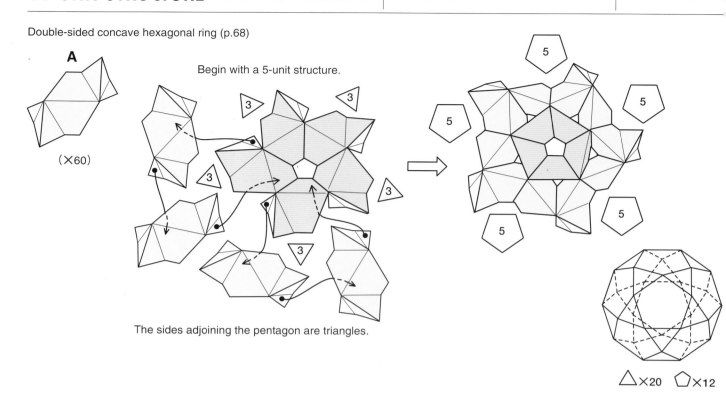

A

（×60）

Begin with a 5-unit structure.

The sides adjoining the pentagon are triangles.

△×20 ⬠×12

Double-sided concave hexagonal ring (p.68)

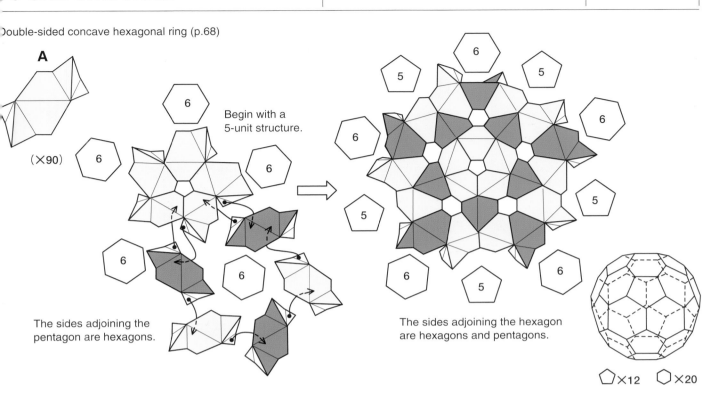

A

(×90)

Begin with a
5-unit structure.

The sides adjoining the
pentagon are hexagons.

The sides adjoining the hexagon
are hexagons and pentagons.

⬠ ×12   ⬡ ×20

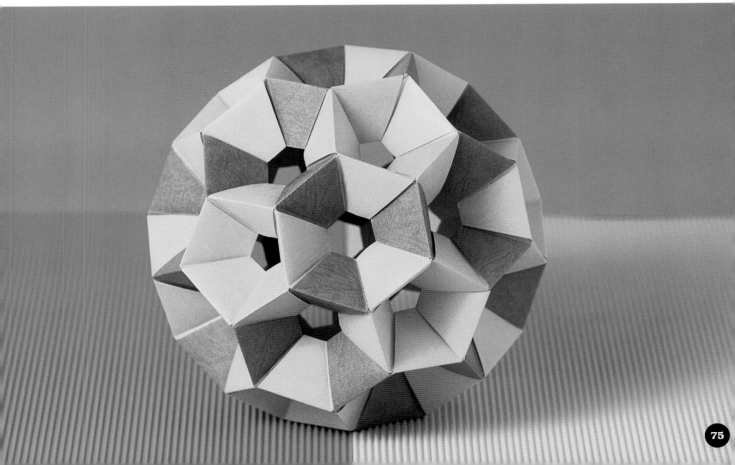

Double-sided concave hexagonal ring (p.68)

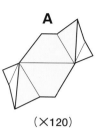

A

（×120）

The sides adjoining the pentagon are squares.
The sides adjoining the triangle are squares.

Begin with a
5-unit structure.

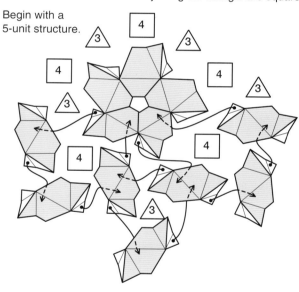

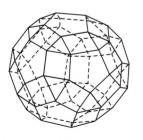

 △×20 □×30 ⬠×12

It is possible to fold double-sided convex and concave units from A4 (210 x 297 mm) or B5 (182 x 257 mm) paper.
In that case, you end up with larger windows.
If you fold using square paper, the windows end up being too large and make the unit fragile.

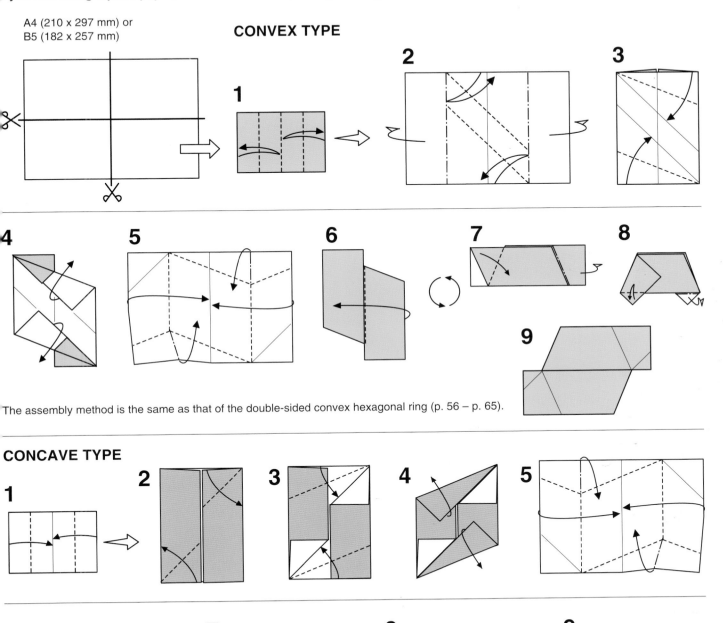

A4 (210 x 297 mm) or
B5 (182 x 257 mm)

CONVEX TYPE

The assembly method is the same as that of the double-sided convex hexagonal ring (p. 56 – p. 65).

CONCAVE TYPE

The assembly method is the same as that of double-sided concave solids (p. 69 – p. 76).

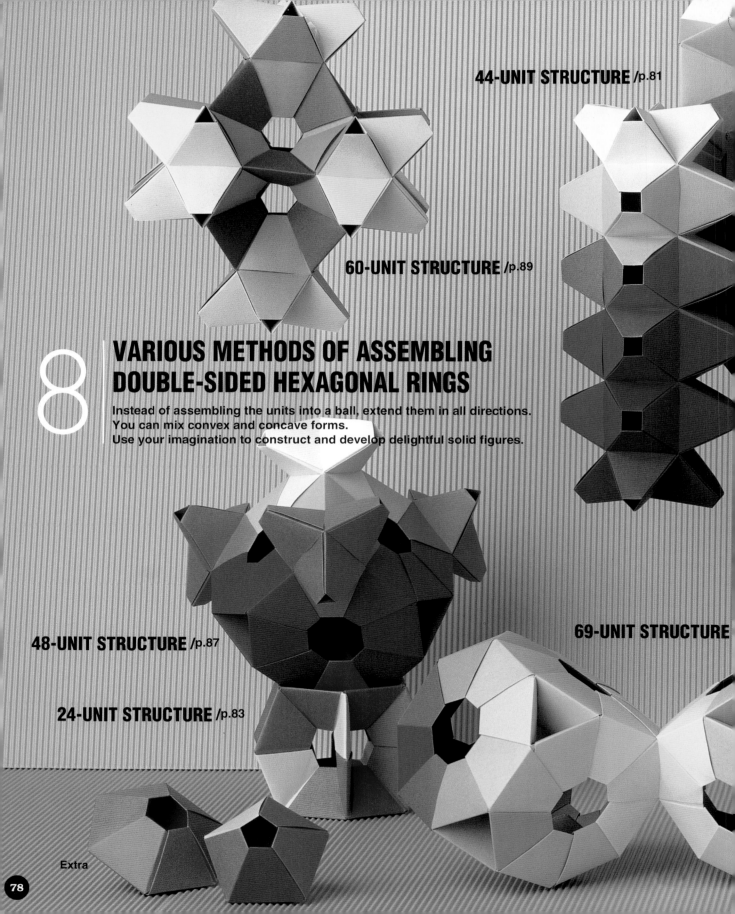

44-UNIT STRUCTURE /p.81

60-UNIT STRUCTURE /p.89

8 VARIOUS METHODS OF ASSEMBLING DOUBLE-SIDED HEXAGONAL RINGS

Instead of assembling the units into a ball, extend them in all directions.
You can mix convex and concave forms.
Use your imagination to construct and develop delightful solid figures.

69-UNIT STRUCTURE

48-UNIT STRUCTURE /p.87

24-UNIT STRUCTURE /p.83

Extra

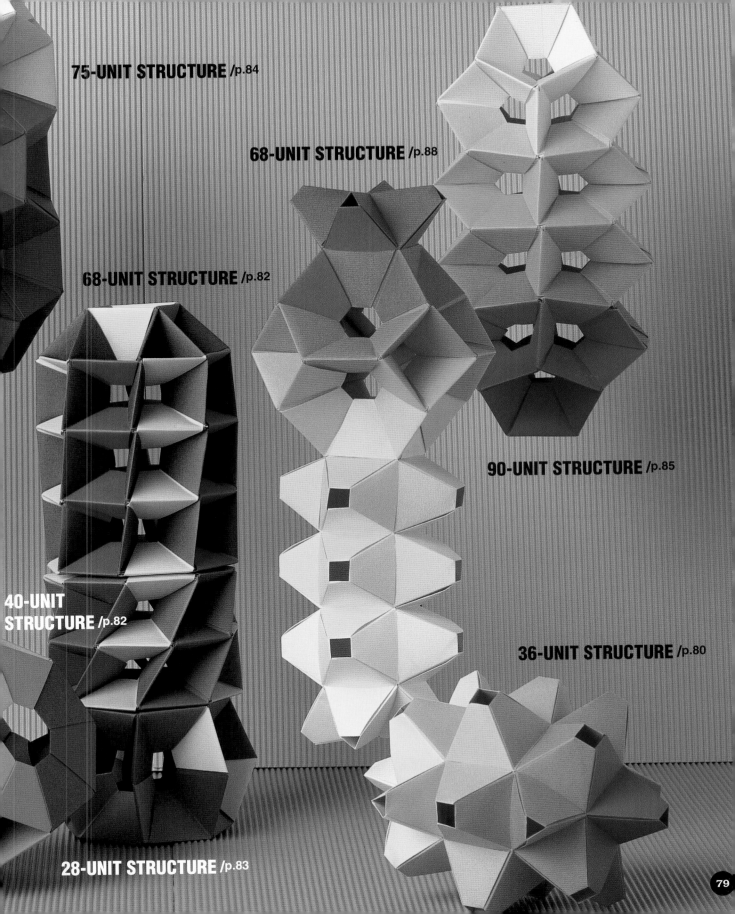

75-UNIT STRUCTURE /p.84

68-UNIT STRUCTURE /p.88

68-UNIT STRUCTURE /p.82

90-UNIT STRUCTURE /p.85

40-UNIT STRUCTURE /p.82

36-UNIT STRUCTURE /p.80

28-UNIT STRUCTURE /p.83

36-UNIT STRUCTURE

level ★★

12cm × 6cm

Double-sided convex
hexagonal ring (p. 54)

(×36)

You can assemble the double-sided hexagonal ring in shapes other than a ball.
See how many kinds of structures you can assemble using convex units.

[Framework Shape]

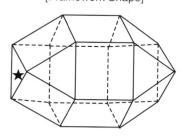

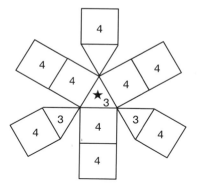

The framework shape viewed lengthwise.
(Intermediate stage)

★

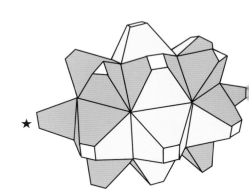

44-UNIT STRUCTURE | level ★★ | 12cm × 6cm

Double-sided convex hexagonal ring (p. 54)

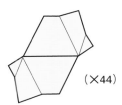

(×44)

[Framework Shape]

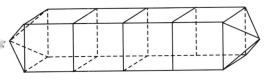

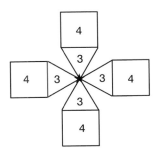

The framework shape viewed lengthwise.
(Intermediate stage)

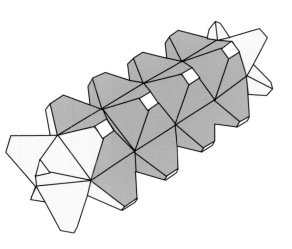

Double-sided concave hexagonal ring (p.68)

The twisted structures, which use different units, were created by Mihoko Tachibana

[Framework Shape]

A   **B**

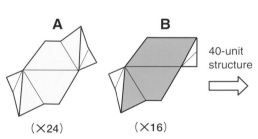

(×24)   (×16)

40-unit
structure

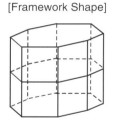

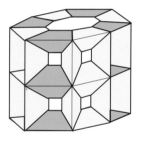

A   **B**

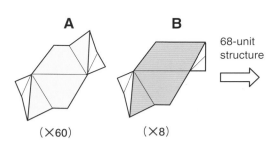

(×60)   (×8)

68-unit
structure

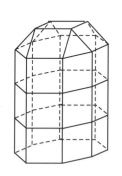

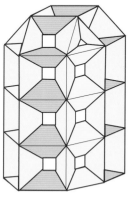

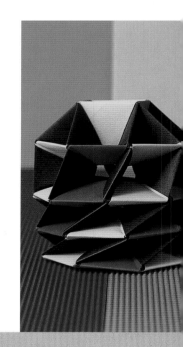

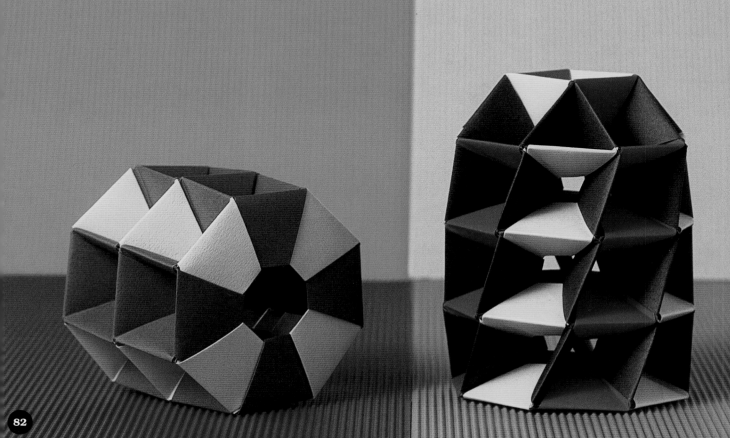

24-UNIT STRUCTURE, 28-UNIT STRUCTURE

level ★★ | 12cm × 6cm

ouble-sided concave hexagonal ring (p.68)

B is made of 2 units.

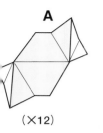

A

（×12）

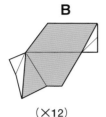

B

（×12）

24-unit structure

[Framework Shape]

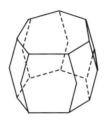

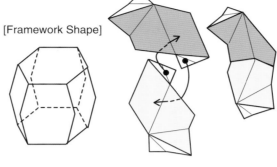

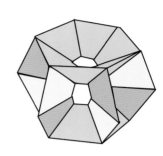

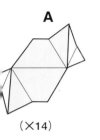

A

（×14）

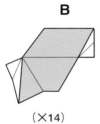

B

（×14）

28-unit structure

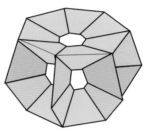

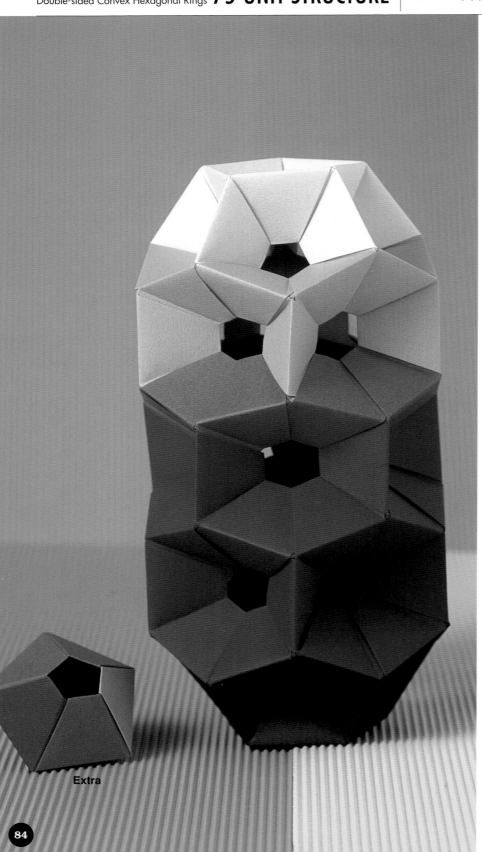

Extra

Double-sided concave
hexagonal ring (p.68)

A

（×75）

[Framework Shape]

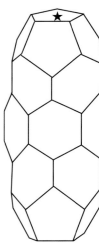

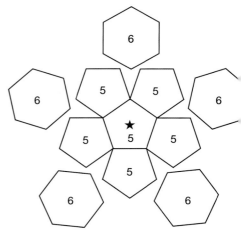

The framework shape viewed lengthwise.
(Intermediate stage)

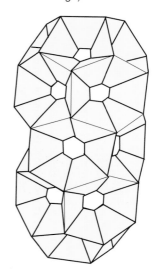

90-UNIT STRUCTURE | level ★★★ | 12cm × 6cm

Double-sided concave
hexagonal ring (p.68)

A

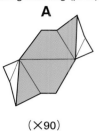

（×90）

[Framework Shape]

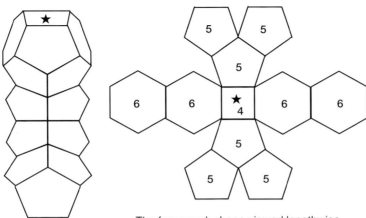

The framework shape viewed lengthwise.
(Intermediate stage)

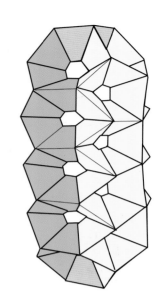

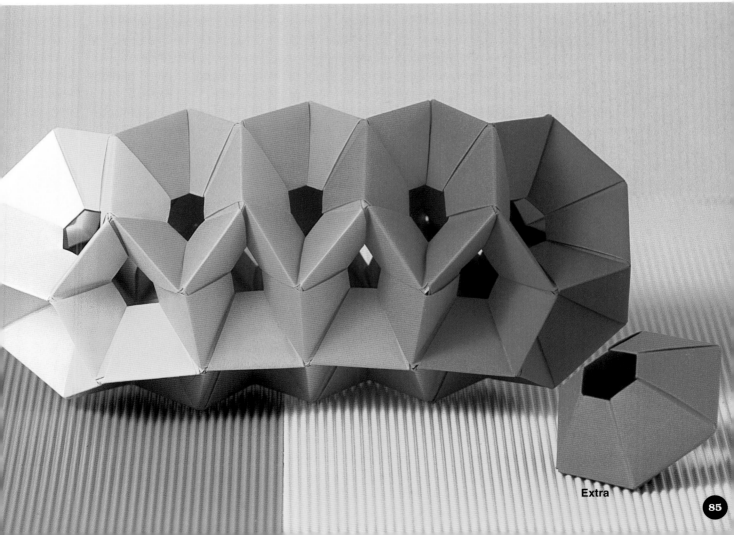

Extra

69-UNIT STRUCTURE

level ★★ | 12cm×6cm

Double-sided convex hexagonal ring (p.5◄

A

（×3）

Double-sided concave hexagonal ring (p.6◄

B   **C**

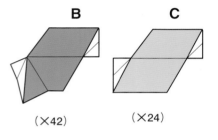

（×42）   （×24）

[Core Solid]

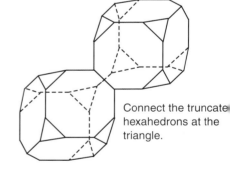

Connect the truncate
hexahedrons at the
triangle.

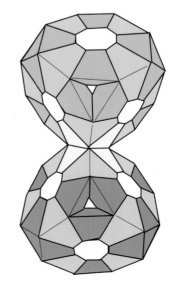

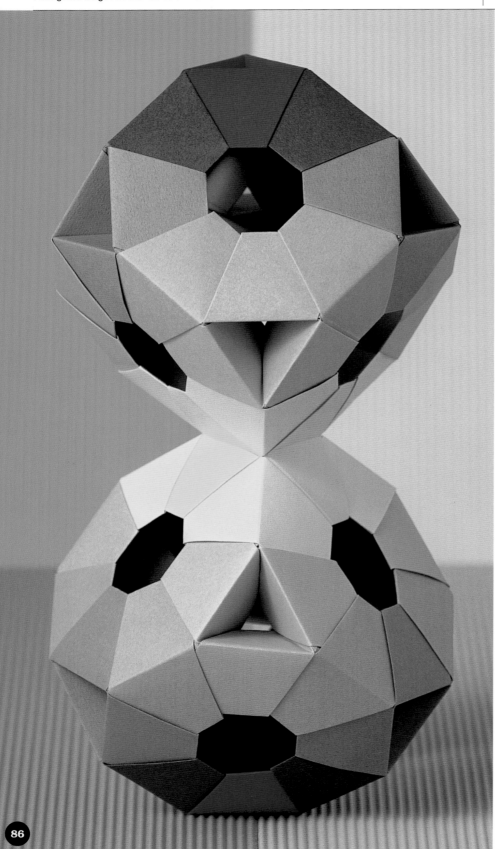

Double-sided convex hexagonal ring (p.54)

A

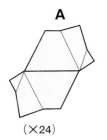

(×24)

Double-sided concave hexagonal ring (p.68)

B   **C**

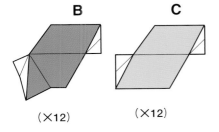

(×12)   (×12)

[Core Solid]

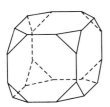

Connect the 3-unit assemblies at the
triangle of truncated hexahedrons.

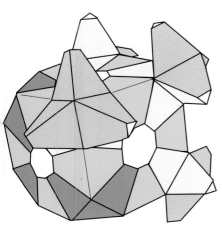

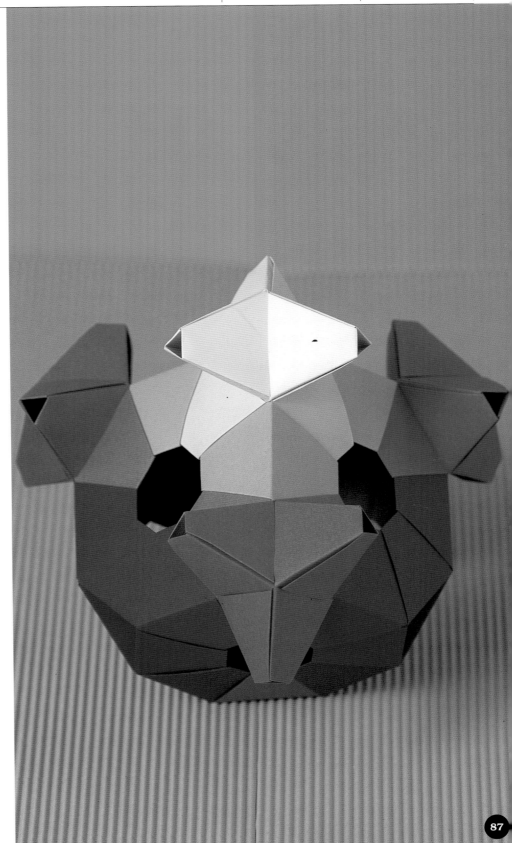

68-UNIT STRUCTURE | level ★★ | 12cm×6cm

If you use convex units for jointing, you can connect solids made of concave units. Devise your own variations and try to construct different shapes. You can figure out how to make forms other than spherical shapes.

Double-sided convex hexagonal ring (p.54)

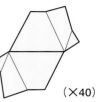

(×40)

Double-sided concave hexagonal ring (p.68)

B   **C**

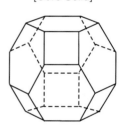

(×16)   (×12)

[Core Solid]

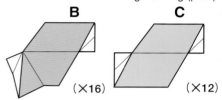

Connect the double-sided convex hexagonal rings to the square.

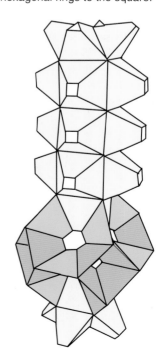

Double-sided convex
hexagonal ring (p.54)

Double-sided concave
hexagonal ring (p.68)

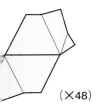

C

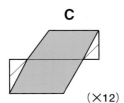

(×48)

(×12)

Six-unit structure of
double-sided convex
hexagonal rings.
The bottom is square.

[Core Solid]

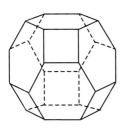

Connect 8-unit assemblies of double-sided
convex hexagonal rings at the square.

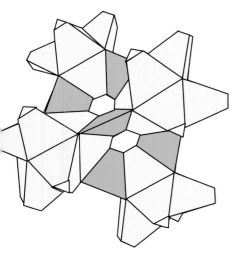

89

9 DIAGONALLY FOLDED TRIANGULAR-UNIT SOLIDS

This unit is made from rectangular paper, which is made from square paper cut in half, with a basic crease made diagonally. The finished solids are sturdy.
Shown here are models with polyhedrons at their core.

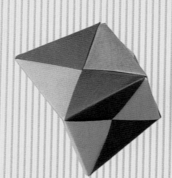

6-UNIT STRUCTURE /p.94

30-UNIT STRUCTURE /p.95

24-UNIT STRUCTURE /p.96

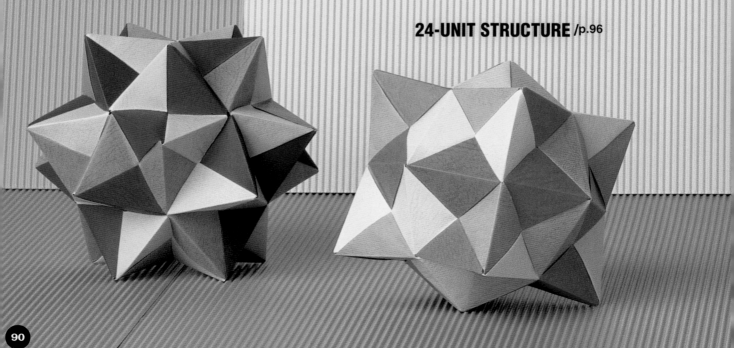

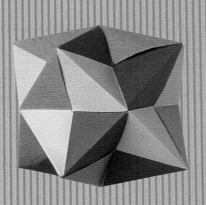

12-UNIT STRUCTURE /p.94

48-UNIT STRUCTURE /p.97

60-UNIT STRUCTURE /p.98

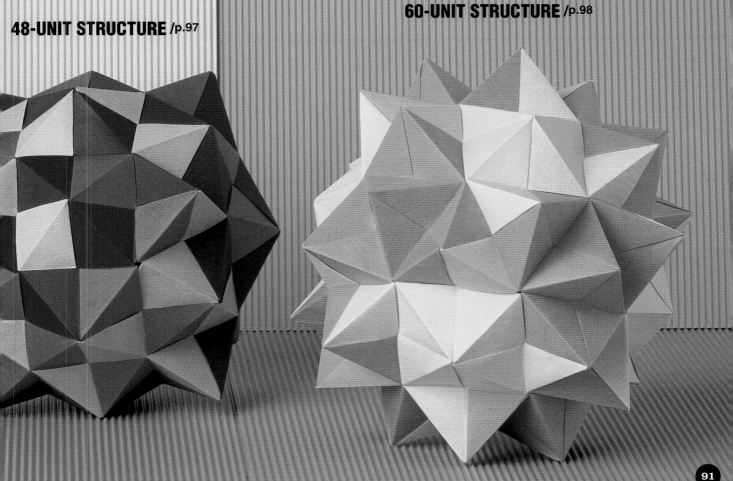

DIAGONALLY FOLDED TRIANGULAR UNIT level ★★ 12cm✕6cm

The hooks on the unit make the solid as sturdy as the double-sided hexagonal ring.
It is easier to fold than you might think.

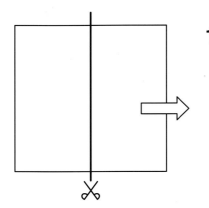

1

2

3

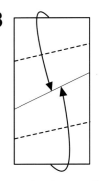

Fold both edges to align
with the diagonal line.

4

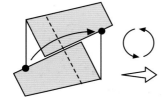

5

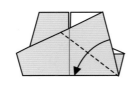

6 Fold backward and
unfold the flap.

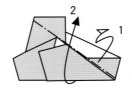

7

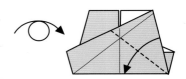

8

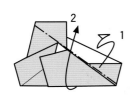

9 Make creases.

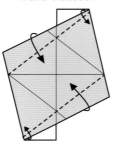

Crush the corners as you like.

10

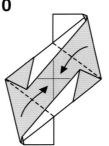

11

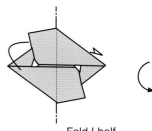

Fold I half.

12

13

Fold triangles.

14

15

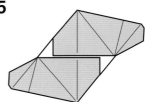

92

Insert the shaded part deep into the slit of the other unit. The tip works as a hook and makes the structure sturdy.

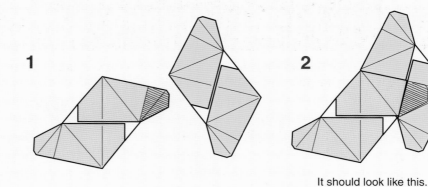

1

2

It should look like this.

3-unit structure

4-unit structure

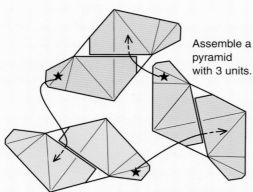

Assemble a pyramid with 3 units.

Insert the parts marked ★ deep into the other units.

Assemble a pyramid with 4 units.

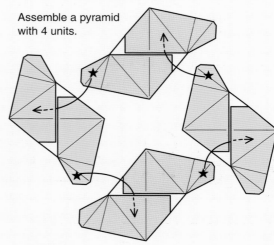

HINT ON ASSEMBLY **2**

The bottom of each element is a triangle or a square, and each pyramid stands on it. This element lets you assemble a variety of solids. The double-sided convex hexagonal ring (p. 54) had a window on top, but these pyramids have no windows. The assembly method is the same as that of the double-sided convex hexagonal ring, but the slope of the top triangle is so gentle that you cannot assemble five-sided or six-sided pyramids.

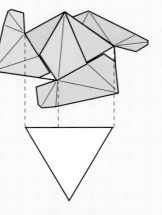

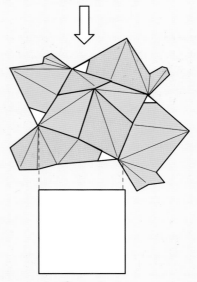

Equilateral triangle
(Triangular pyramid)

Square
(Square pyramid)

6-UNIT STRUCTURE Regular Tetrahedron Star, 12-UNIT STRUCTURE Regular Octahedron Star | level ★ | 12cm×6cm

Triangle Unit (p. 92)

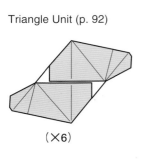

(×6)

Begin with a
3-unit structure.

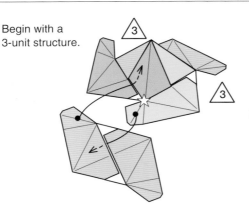

Regular Tetrahedron Star

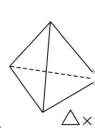

Three triangular pyramids join at the star.

△×

Triangle Unit (p. 92)

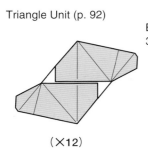

(×12)

Begin with a
3-unit structure.

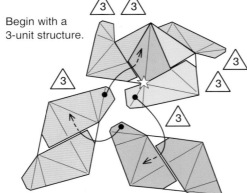

Regular Octahedron Star

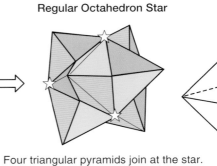

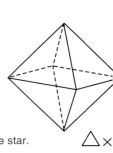

Four triangular pyramids join at the star.

△×

Triangle Unit (p. 92)

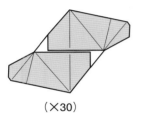

（×30）

egin with a
unit structure.

Five triangular pyramids join at the star.

⬇

Regular Icosahedron Star

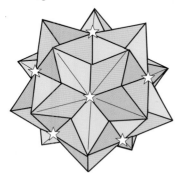

Five triangular pyramids gather at the star.

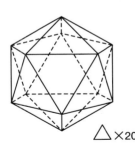

△×20

24-UNIT STRUCTURE Cuboctahedron Star | **level ★★** | 12cm×6cm

Triangular Unit (p. 92)

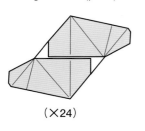

(×24)

Begin with a 4-unit structure.

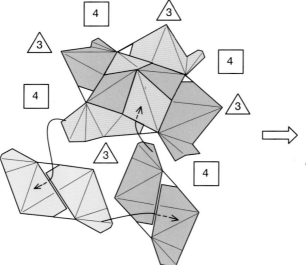

Cuboctahedron Star

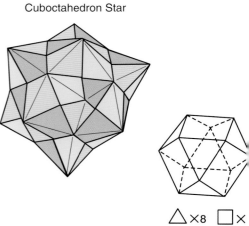

△×8 □×

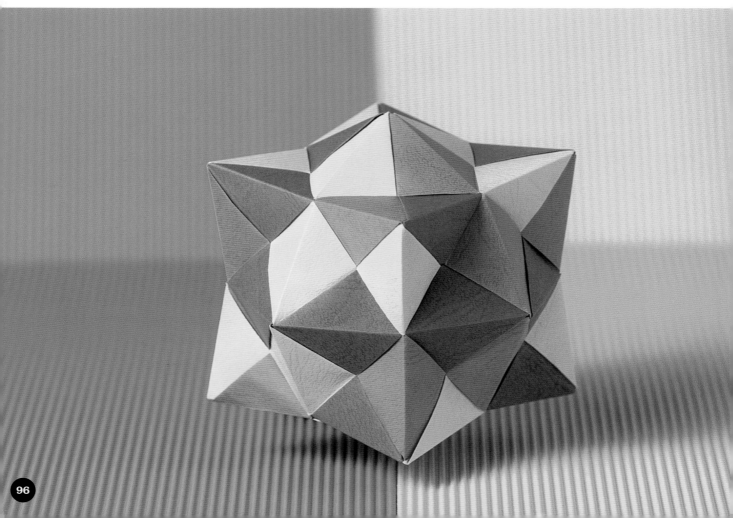

8-UNIT STRUCTURE Rhombic Cuboctahedron Star | **level ★★** | 12cm×6cm

Triangular Unit (p. 92)

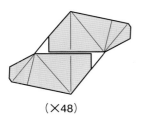

(×48)

egin with a
 unit structure.

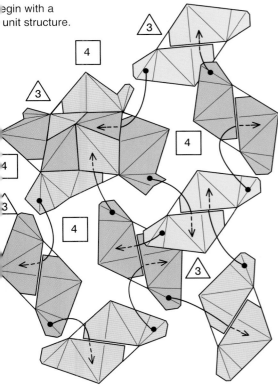

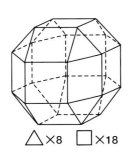

△×8 □×18

60-UNIT STRUCTURE Variant Cube Star | level ★★★

Triangle Unit (p. 92)

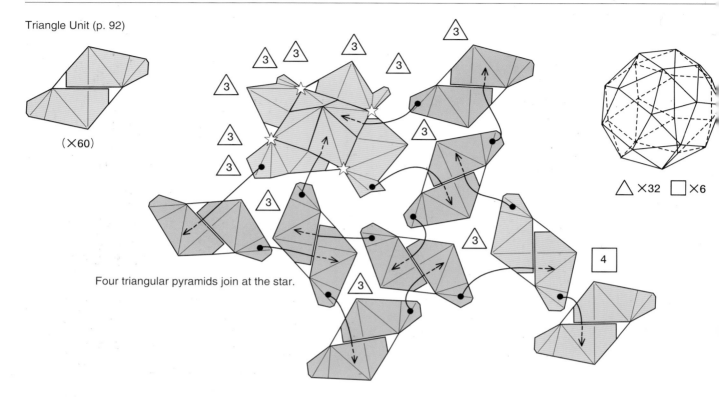

(×60)

Four triangular pyramids join at the star.

△×32 □×6